Lemon v. Kurtzman

The Religion and Public Funds Case

Leah Farish

Landmark Supreme Court Cases

Enslow Publishers, Inc.

40 Industrial Road	PO Box 38
Box 398	Aldershot
Berkeley Heights, NJ 07922	Hants GU12 6BP
USA	UK

http://www.enslow.com

Library of Congress Cataloging-in-Publication Data

Farish, Leah.
      Lemon v. Kurtzman: the religion and public funds case / Leah Farish.
         p. cm. — (Landmark Supreme Court cases)
      Includes bibliographical references and index.
      Summary: Discusses the details and impact of the Supreme Court's decision
in Lemon v. Kurtzman, which was about the use of public funds in connection
with religion.
      ISBN 0-7660-1339-1
        1. Lemon, Alton—Trials, litigation, etc.—Juvenile literature. 2. Pennsylvania-
Trials, litigation, etc.—Juvenile literature. 3. Education—Finance—law and
legislation—Pennsylvania—Juvenile literature. 4. Education—Finance—Law and
legislation—United States—Juvenile literature. 5. Church and state—United
States—Juvenile literature. [1. Lemon, Alton—Trials, litigation, etc.
2. Education—Finance—Law and legislation. 3. Church and state.] I. Title: Lemon
versus Kurtzman. II. Title: Lemon vs. Kurtzman. III. Title. IV. Series.

KF228.L46 F37   2000
344.73'076—dc21

                                     99-040316

Printed in the United States of America

10 9 8 7 6 5 4 3 2

To Our Readers: We have done our best to make sure all Internet addresses in this book were
active and appropriate when we went to press. However, the author and the publisher have no
control over and assume no liability for the material available on those Internet sites or on
other Web sites they may link to. Any comments or suggestions can be sent by e-mail to
comments@enslow.com or to the address on the back cover.

Photo Credits: Corbis/Bettmann-UPI, p. 11; Corel Corporation, p. 41; Harris &
Ewing, Collection of the Supreme Court of the United States, p. 49; Leah Farish,
pp. 13, 28, 36, 56, 83, 90, 103; Leslie Rea, p. 66; Library of Congress, p. 17;
Painting by Gilbert Stuart, Courtesy Bowdoin College Museum of Art, Reproduced
from the Dictionary of American Portraits published by Dover Publications, Inc.,
1967, p. 22; United States House of Representatives, p. 99.

Cover Photo: Ronnie Kaufman/The Stock Market (menorah); Ariel Skelley/The
Stock Market (nativity)

Contents

1

Close Questions

The *Lemon* v. *Kurtzman* case is about the use of public funds in connection with religion. *Lemon* v. *Kurtzman* is based on the Establishment Clause, a part of the First Amendment to the Constitution. This Amendment provides in part that "Congress shall make no law respecting an establishment of religion, or prohibiting the free exercise thereof. . . ." This part of the Constitution is at the heart of many disputes over the relationship of government to religion. This may seem like an abstract problem, but if you are in school, your life has already been affected by the *Lemon* case.

Here are some situations where the issues raised in the *Lemon* case have resurfaced:

• A public elementary school announced that a totem pole would be erected on the school grounds. A ceremony would be held to commemorate this and "prayers would be offered to Mother Earth."[1] Parents protested that the ceremony was an establishment of religion, and the plans were changed to avoid religious overtones.

• A few boys who were being taught at home for religious reasons wanted to be able to participate in the band and sports activities of their local public school. "It's only fair that if the parents pay taxes, they should be able to avail themselves of some of the public schooling they pay for," said their attorney.[2] The students were barred anyway.

• Deaf children who needed special help, such as speech therapy, attended a private religious school. The school wanted to have tax-funded teachers come and help the children. It was argued, however, that doing so would benefit religion and thus violate the Establishment Clause of the First Amendment.[3]

The part of the First Amendment with which the *Lemon* case dealt is the first several words. Those words provide that government may not establish, or set up, a national religion. When the public's money, received from taxes, is used to promote or help any religion, a danger exists of setting up a national religion. If public funds assist a private, religious school, a violation of the Establishment Clause of the First Amendment can occur. But there are gray areas—matters of degree—that have given rise to vigorous debate. Are the three previous examples instances of an establishment of religion? What about when a city allows a religious display on city property? Or when a student prays at graduation? Is the teaching of evolution an establishment of antireligious philosophy? How much money from the government is too much? How much involvement of religion with politics is too much? Each question leads to more questions, often made difficult by passionate opinions on all sides.

As one Supreme Court Justice once said about church-state relations, "deep feelings are aroused."[4] It is not just the state [that is, government] that must avoid too much linkage with religion out of respect for the First Amendment. Many Christians and others believe they cannot safely be too involved with the government. Some examples of this caution are seen as warnings in the New Testament, "No one can serve two masters," and "Render unto Caesar what is Caesar's, and unto God what is God's."[5]

The Roman Catholic doctrines about the Pope create a certain amount of tension, too. As one Catholic leader said, "The world is afraid of us because we have a Pope. It can't count on us because our loyalties are divided."[6] Whether it is an American Indian who wants to smoke peyote as a traditional ritual, a religious group that loses its tax-exempt status for endorsing political candidates, a Seventh-Day Adventist who refuses to work on her Saturday Sabbath, a Jehovah's Witness who will not let his child receive a blood transfusion due to religious beliefs, or an atheist who believes her child will be psychologically harmed by hearing a teacher say a prayer, emotions run high when religion and public life cross paths, and sparks may fly. This was never more likely than in the era when the *Lemon* case arose.

Lemon v. *Kurtzman*, handed down in 1971, has given us a three-part test by which to analyze the appropriateness of church/state relations. Briefly, it allows church/state relations that:

- have a secular purpose (that is, a nonreligious purpose such as public safety or convenience);

- neither inhibit nor advance religion, and;

- do not cause government and religion to become "entangled" with each other.

This test can be applied to school-funding disputes

and to many other kinds of fact settings to check for an establishment of religion. The test is still often used today, though we will see that it has also been rejected in some cases and added to in others. The issue of church-state relations is a complicated one.

The tumultuous 1960s included the assassinations of Robert Kennedy and Martin Luther King, Jr. The Vietnam War, having cost the lives of many thousands of Americans by then, was still troubling many people. Every male high school senior had memorized his draft number, which might call him to war. President Richard Nixon was perhaps at the height of his power, with the Watergate scandal yet to come. It was a tense time, and schools felt it.

Prayer, Bible reading, and the posting of the Ten Commandments in public schools had all been rejected in the courts. Teachers, parents, and principals tried to figure out how to incorporate these rejections into their daily lives. Would they be sued if they allowed a moment of silence? What if they taught biblical accounts of Creation in science class along with evolution? Could college students have prayer groups on campus? What about football players who wanted to start their games with a prayer? And must teachers stop praying individually with students during free time? Suddenly, very routine or time-honored activities became a minefield of possible lawsuits for schools. "We didn't know what we could do, or what would get us fired," said one public school teacher in 1970.

> Sex education was also starting to be introduced in the classroom, and there were clashes of values over that as well. Observers from all over the place would come into my classroom; I often didn't even know what they were watching for. I just did the best I could.[7]

To add to the challenge, the free speech rights of students had been resoundingly affirmed in 1969. In *Tinker* v. *Des Moines*, the Supreme Court had been presented with several middle school and high school students who wore black armbands to their public school to protest American involvement in Vietnam. School officials had forbidden this, saying that they feared some kind of disturbance if such symbols were allowed, though there had been none up to that point in their schools. The Court had rejected this abstract fear. It held that unless evidence of actual disruption was shown, such as fighting or interference with classroom teaching, both teachers and students kept their rights to free expression while at school.[8] No one knew how much disruption on public school grounds might erupt as students tested their rights. At the college level, however, demonstrations had led to mass marches and burning buildings.

In *Tinker* v. *Des Moines* in 1969, the Supreme Court affirmed students' free speech rights, after several students wore black armbands to school to protest American involvement in the Vietnam War. Despite fears that the armbands would cause a disturbance, school officials were prevented from prohibiting student expression.

Integration, the process of admitting all races of children to the same public schools, had been implemented nationwide. Unrest over the idea of blacks and whites in the same classrooms had pretty much dissolved. However, many were bothered by the fact that the Supreme Court had forced this change on them. One senator had said that the *Brown* v. *Board of Education* decision, which began the process of racial integration in the schools, was "the most serious blow that has yet been struck against the rights of the states."[9] Just the year before *Lemon* came to the Supreme Court, Justice Abe Fortas had resigned from the Supreme Court amid allegations of working under improper influence from financial interests. Congressman Gerald Ford sought the impeachment of another Justice, William O. Douglas, in April 1970. Though that effort was unsuccessful, one might say the Court was the subject of an unusual amount of criticism.[10] The Justices do not talk much with the press and are expected to keep a low profile in their private lives. As such, not much could be done directly to seek the support or confidence of the American public.

Into all this we can add one more factor that made *Lemon*'s outcome uncertain—a brand-new Chief Justice. Taking over in 1969 from an aggressive predecessor, the new leader of the Supreme Court,

A public school teacher reads to students. Very routine or time-honored activities became a minefield of possible lawsuits for schools.

Warren Burger, was widely expected to deliver a much more restrained set of rulings. Even President Nixon told everyone that that was the reason he had appointed Burger.[11] Fulfilling these expectations would mean shifting the whole direction of the Court. Burger himself was "personally critical of the media and extremely sensitive to press criticism."[12] A person in his shoes might be eager to please. But, in the splintered society of 1970, please whom?

2

The Evolution of American Education

Early American schools reflected the background of Europeans, particularly the English who colonized America. They were originally influenced only by the Christian religion. Now, however, they reflect the diversity of the population of the United States, with its many kinds of beliefs. Private schools (that is, schools funded without tax support) may teach and require beliefs ranging from Islam to atheism, but the Supreme Court has ruled that religion has a limited place in public, or tax-supported, schools.

Schools in England during the 1500s and 1600s were available to the wealthy, but under the so-called Poor Laws of 1563 and 1601, unemployed people from ages twelve to sixty were required to enter an apprenticeship—an environment in which they would learn a trade. There was no rule against teaching religion at taxpayer expense, but the apprenticeships focused on the basic skills needed to practice a trade. In 1774, Empress Maria-Teresa set up state schools in the Austro-Hungarian Empire, teaching Catholicism as part of the curriculum.[1] Settlers who came to our continent from Europe taught their children at home or in groups as their time permitted, and sometimes shared a teacher, who might be a parent or a single person.[2] In such settings, they had complete freedom to teach whatever they wanted, and diligently taught religion. Towns or private individuals gave the land or buildings needed for schools, and costs were covered by local taxes and by tuition (fees) paid by those who could afford it.[3]

The Massachusetts Bay Colony passed a law in 1647 that said, in part:

> It being one chiefe project of that old deluder, Sathan, to keepe men from the knowledge of the scriptures, as in former time. . . . It is therefore ordered . . . [that] after the Lord hath increased [the settlement to fifty households, they] shall then forthwith appointe one within their towne, to teach all such children as shall resorte to him, to write and read. . . . And it is further ordered, That where any towne shall increase to the number of one hundred families . . . they shall sett up

A public school classroom in early America is shown here. Students of varying ages were all taught in the same single classroom by one teacher.

a grammar schoole . . . to instruct youths, so farr as they may bee fitted for the university.[4]

About 130 years later, in the late 1700s and early 1800s, Noah Webster, called "America's Schoolmaster," was writing history books, spellers, dictionaries, and other texts and working to support schools with taxes. He wanted to make sure that "young persons . . . early understand that the genuine source of correct . . . [civic] principles is the Bible, particularly the New Testament or the Christian religion."[5] William McGuffey's Readers, first printed in 1836, were full of passages from the Bible, and he stated that "[i]n a Christian country, that man is to be pitied, who, at this day, can honestly object to the imbuing the minds of youth with the language and spirit of the Word of God."[6]

Some were sensing the problems with government endorsement of religion, though little was written of it in relation to schools. James Madison helped write the First Amendment to the Constitution. He favored a principle of government not supporting religion and religion not supporting government.[7] He warned dramatically that any other approach

will be found to leave crevices at least thro' which bigotry may introduce persecution; a monster, that feeding and thriving on its own venom, gradually swells to a size and strength overwhelming all laws divine & human.[8]

In other words, a government-supported Church had become a menace to those in England, and he dreaded the same thing happening here. However, he wrote little on the role of religion in education.

Thomas Jefferson was the third president of the United States. He is often seen as someone who opposed government teaching of religion. However, he also founded the University of Virginia with the regulation that "religious sects" or groups could establish "schools" on the campus. In addition, students of such "schools, . . . if they attend any school of the University, shall be considered as students of the University, subject to the same regulations, and entitled to the same rights and privileges."[9] He also served as superintendent of the District of Columbia public school system when its required texts were a Bible and a hymnal.

Another founder of the nation was Governeur Morris, the senator who actually wrote down the Constitution. He said, "[E]ducation should teach the precepts of religion, and the duties of man towards God."[10] Most other leaders who founded our nation agreed that religion and public life could mix in varying degrees, and many agreed that religious elements even in tax-supported education were desirable. For example, article three of the Northwest Ordinance of 1787, in setting aside land for schools, said, "Religion, morality, and knowledge being necessary to good government and the happiness of mankind, schools and the means of education shall forever be encouraged."[11]

The various Christian religions did not take identical approaches to schooling their children. Catholics and Anglicans felt that education was a private matter, and looked to church and family to perform this function, including educating girls for their expected roles as homemakers and boys for careers. Quakers stressed basic literacy for all, including girls, African Americans, and American Indians. Presbyterians and other denominations from the Protestant Reformation emphasized the value of hard work and of understanding church doctrine, especially for boys. They taught their Scriptures, however, to all who would listen, as a means of spreading their faith.[12]

Common Schools and the Melting Pot

In the 1800s, the arrival in the United States of settlers from all over the world and the growth of industry created a demand for common schools. These schools would give even poor children equal opportunity by providing a minimum level of free education. Horace Mann was one of the leaders in the common school movement who did not propose to teach any particular church's faith. He favored instead a general Christian ethic of honesty, effort, and respect for reason. Catholics and some private schools took a dim view of this movement. They feared that it gave government too much control in indoctrinating children. Others believed their cultural distinctions might get lost in such a "melting pot" of cultures coming together. Still others said that it was not the job of government to educate children with tax money.[13]

Two factors increased the demand for public help with educating children: first, in the latter half of the 1800s, our economy needed more and more skilled workers; second, the thinly settled West could not always generate private funds and teachers in frontier communities. However, while most Americans agreed on the use of taxes to pay for elementary schools, funding high schools was controversial. The United States Supreme Court eventually held that states could raise taxes to pay for public high schools. The National Education Association (NEA) is a group of public-school teachers and administrators that aims to improve public education and classroom conditions. The organization urged that high school should be a time for deep studies of the classics in Greek and Latin, and in Western history and the Bible.[14] Educators such as

University of Virginia founder Thomas Jefferson said that "religious sects" or groups could establish "schools" on the campus of the university.

John Dewey, promoted "life adjustment education," and wanted high schools to emphasize more practical skills.[15]

Both approaches agreed that public funds could be used for schooling from first through twelfth grade. Government aid to schools that were not public, however, was problematic. Some communities *did* provide money for private schools to run school buses or buy textbooks. Catholics were beginning to be upset by the reading of the Protestant King James Bible in public schools. In New York, they requested public funds for their parish, or parochial, schools. There was even fighting in the streets over the issue on one or two occasions.[16] In 1876, Congress came within two votes of amending the Constitution to bar states from aiding religious schools.[17] As the twentieth century arrived, it appeared that the courts would decide whether private schools could be assisted by the government, and on what terms public schools could allow religion within their doors.

One of the first rumblings of the century came from Brooklyn, New York, in 1906. There, Jewish parents complained that Christmas festivities offended them, and they took their children out of school for most of December. A few years later, some conservative Protestants objected to tax-funded schools teaching evolution, which they felt left God out of science classes.[18] It was becoming harder to keep everyone satisfied.

Jewish Americans have consistently been supportive of public schools, and have seen them as "crucial to integrating the Jewish immigrants into the culture at the turn of the [20th] century."[19] To supplement what their children were learning at school, Jewish families and synagogues gave religious instruction in Hebrew, using the Old Testament and other texts important to their faith.[20] But later, some parents wanted an hour or so per week to be taken from the regular public school day to allow time to go elsewhere for religious instruction. This was held permissible under the First Amendment in *Zorach* v. *Clauson* as a so-called released-time class, which will be discussed further in Chapter 7.[21]

Challenges to Religion in the Schools

The average public-school day included school-led religious practice. About one third of schools in 1900 began the school day with the Lord's Prayer or other prayer, and three fourths of them allowed teachers to read the Bible to classes. Objecting parents were normally allowed "excusal" of their children.[22] Some parents, however, felt that having their children excused from religious exercises made their children outcasts, or "oddballs."[23] The first lawsuit against the schools for "establishing a religion" was *Engel* v. *Vitale*.[24] There, the Supreme Court reversed all three levels of the New York state court system and struck down a brief prayer that was composed and read by public school officials. The decision was highly unpopular and failed to cite any cases or laws as precedent. Reactions of religious and government leaders included the following statements about the case and those who decided it: It "shocked and frightened" some; it amounted to "tampering with America's soul"; and "they're driving God out."[25] Some predicted that *Engel* "would strengthen those who wanted federal aid for private schools, [and] give middle-class parents one more reason to take their children out of urban school. . . ."[26]

However, that was not the last of the changes. Atheist Madalyn Murray O'Hair and some other parents challenged a public school practice of daily Bible reading. Said O'Hair, "We find the Bible to be nauseating, historically inaccurate, replete with the ravings of madmen. We find God to be sadistic, brutal, and a representation of hatred. . . ."[27] The Court did not adopt these views. However, in *Abington* v. *Schempp* it *did* hold that no part of the official public school day can be devoted to Bible reading, other than in the context of study of the Bible's literary or historical aspects.[28]

This is still the law with the exception of student-led religious clubs, being allowed to meet on campuses. (This exception will be discussed in Chapter 7.)

What's All the Fuss About?

So was it not obvious to religious parents that Bible reading and prayer could not be conducted by government officials? Is that not the end of the matter? No, because there are two additional considerations: the free exercise of religion also guaranteed by the First Amendment, and the right of parents to direct the education of their children.

The Free Exercise of Religion

Children do have freedom of conscience and expression even when they are at school, and tax-supported schools must honor those rights by not requiring a particular religious belief or worship activity by a student. (Private schools can.) For example, a student is free to discuss religion—or atheism, the belief that God does not exist—pray openly, or choose religious subjects for assignments if these things are not disruptive of the school day and curriculum.[29] Students can refuse to attend assemblies or engage in performances, meditation, or other activities that violate sincere religious or antireligious beliefs. The First Amendment guarantees that the state cannot violate a person's conscience: "Congress shall make no law respecting an establishment of religion, or *prohibiting the free exercise thereof.*" (italics added) "Congress" has been expanded to mean cities, states, school districts, and all government agencies. On the other hand, the Founding Fathers did not intend that we should never hear new or even disagreeable ideas. Although children should not be forced, subtly or openly, to serve a Christian God or a Muslim Allah or any other God, for that matter, they must learn to live alongside a variety of philosophical strangers. Even debating and arguing about truth and myth can be a useful mental exercise and a path to important answers for some young people. As Samuel Adams, called the Father of the American Revolution, once said, "I am not a bigot. I can hear a . . . man pray who is at the same time a friend of his country."[30]

Parental Rights

Education has almost universally been seen as the duty of parents, who now usually delegate most formal instruction to teachers. As early as the 1640s, American colonists passed laws requiring, in part ". . . all masters of families do once a week [at the least] catechize their children and servants in the grounds and principles of

In public school classrooms in the early 1950s, elaborate Christmas decorations were common.

Religion," and teach them to read and understand the Bible and the laws of the community.[31]

But as laws were passed requiring all children to go to school (compulsory attendance statutes), the freedom of parents not to send their children to government schools naturally came into question. The Supreme Court, before it decided *Lemon* v. *Kurtzman,* had to decide these basic issues. And of course, it is usually adults, not children, who decide to hire lawyers and sue school districts, so the rights of parents become a matter of practical importance.

One of the first cases about parents' rights was *Maynard* v. *Hill,* which in 1888 held that the duty of a parent to a child included that of education. The Supreme Court there based this on "natural law" and on "the implied obligation which parents assume in entering into wedlock, and by bringing children into the world."[32] During the 1920s, three significant cases established the freedom of parents to educate their children according to their consciences. First was a situation in which parents wanted their child to be taught German. Due in part to the political climate of World War I, there was anti-German sentiment sufficient to forbid this. But the Court made essential the "right of an individual to marry, establish a home, and bring up children" in the way the parents see fit.[33]

Two years later, the Court pursued this thought in a case called *Pierce* v. *Society of Sisters*. Here a group of private schools sued because a state law made almost any private elementary or middle school illegal. The Court struck down the law, saying that the law

> unreasonably interferes with the liberty of parents and guardians to direct the upbringing and education of children under their control. The fundamental theory of liberty . . . [forbids] the state to standardize its children by forcing them to accept instruction from public teachers only. The child is not the mere creature of the State; those who nurture him and direct his destiny have the right, coupled with the high duty, to recognize and prepare him for additional obligations.[34]

These principles were repeated in a case in Hawaii. Japanese parents living there wanted their children's private school to be free of the "Americanizing efforts" of state regulations. The Court sided with the parents, saying that there was a liberty interest on behalf of the parents to determine their children's teachers and schoolbooks without unreasonable state interference.[35]

After this 1927 case, the Court did not have another on this issue for almost fifty years, around the time it decided *Lemon*. At that time, a question arose about whether a state could make it illegal for women to buy birth control devices. The Court there, and in the case that legalized abortion, found a "privacy" interest guaranteed by the Constitution. The word *privacy*, however does not appear anywhere in the Constitution.[36] Some degree of privacy is implied by the Fourth Amendment, which guarantees that our homes are our castles—that "[t]he right of the people to be secure in their persons, houses, papers, and effects, against unreasonable searches and seizures, shall not be violated. . . ." This privacy interest ensures that the decision of how to educate a child belongs to mothers and fathers.

Into the confusion of competing interests stepped the new Chief Justice of the Supreme Court, Warren Burger. He would be called on to help decide whether government funds could be spent on private schools. From the solution he devised, many other questions about the place of the spiritual and the secular world would be addressed if not finally answered.

3

The Lawsuit Begins

The case called *Lemon* v. *Kurtzman* started in a place you may be sitting as you read this book—a school. A parent in Pennsylvania, Alton Lemon, heard that taxes on racetrack tickets were being paid to private schools under a state law providing teachers and materials to religious schools. The state was to closely monitor these secular (nonreligious) courses to make sure that public teachers and texts were not connected to "any subject matter expressing religious teaching, or the morals or forms of worship of any sect."[1] School accounts would be audited by the state auditor general to make sure the funds were not mixed with other money. Lemon decided to consult a lawyer. He thought this plan should be outlawed. The name of Henry W. Sawyer came up. Sawyer was celebrated for winning the famous *Abington* v. *Schempp* case, which had outlawed school-led prayer in the public schools, and he agreed to take the case with Alton Lemon as plaintiff, the one filing suit.

However, the attorney quickly saw a problem. Lemon had never bought a ticket to a horse race, and someone might protest that, therefore, he had no "standing" to sue. Standing is a crucial ingredient in any lawsuit, particularly in a taxpayer protest case, in which it must be proven that he actually had to pay a tax that was somehow unlawful. In fact, some organizations that joined the *Lemon* suit as plaintiffs were dismissed for lack of standing. Sawyer said, "Out of an abundance of caution, I had Mr. Lemon go up and buy a ticket at the racetrack. And hang on to the stub."[2]

They filed a suit alleging, or pleading, that the government had committed a wrong by helping offer the classes and other things to religious people. That plan, they said, violated the First Amendment—specifically, the Establishment Clause, which says that Congress (and later, the fifty states) can not "establish," or promote, religion.

David H. Kurtzman, then superintendent of Public Instruction of the Commonwealth of Pennsylvania, was the defendant, or person being sued, in this case. He was not being sued personally, but rather in his "official capacity." He was represented, among others, by a Christian attorney named William Bentley Ball, who specialized in First Amendment cases. Ball would later call "secularists" such as Lemon "barbarians in Brooks Brothers suits."[3]

The defendants made a motion to dismiss on the pleadings. The motion to dismiss is a legal document filed by the defendant that says that no other answer is necessary—the pleadings do not state an adequate case. The Court held a hearing on the question, using the rule that when pleadings are attacked, every doubt must be resolved in favor of the plaintiff. "It was a very light burden of proof," says Sawyer. Nonetheless, the three-judge panel ruled against Lemon. However, one judge wrote a very articulate dissent. "That should have warned them," said Sawyer.[4] Under the law as it stood at the time, there was no appeal of cases against the state except directly to the United States Supreme Court. So Sawyer filed his appeal. No one had even presented a moment of testimony or a sheet of paper as evidence, but the case was on its way to the United States Supreme Court.

Meanwhile, in Providence, Rhode Island, another controversy was brewing. Joan DiCenso telephoned Milton Stanzler, a lawyer there, for help in contesting a situation similar to that in *Lemon*. A Rhode Island law permitted taxes to add up to 15 percent of whatever a

A religious group sings at Union Station in Washington, D.C. Religious activities can take place on public property under certain circumstances.

teacher was making in a private school. This formula could be used as long as the teacher taught only those subjects that were also offered in public schools and signed an agreement not to teach religion while receiving the tax money. About one fourth of all Rhode Island school children were in private schools, almost all of them Roman Catholic.[5]

Stanzler had started the state chapter of the American Civil Liberties Union (ACLU), a nonpartisan organization devoted to defending the rights and freedoms of the people of the United States, over a decade before. He shared the ACLU's suspicions of links between government and churches. "I was very active at the time," he said. "We decided we wanted to test that issue, and she [DiCenso] volunteered."[6] Stanzler called Leo Pfeffer, whom he considers a "brilliant lawyer," for help. Stanzler said of Pfeffer, "I respected him. I felt I should be following him, rather than he helping me."[7] The defendant, Robinson, testified in the case, but, as in *Lemon*, the plaintiff never did. The three-judge district court granted an injunction, or order stopping the state program, and they, too, had to head to the Supreme Court.

The Final Appeal

When a person wants to be heard before the Supreme Court, he or she must file a petition for *certiorari*, often called cert. *Certiorari* is a Latin word meaning "to be informed of." If a court grants cert, this means it will hear the case. Unlike the lower courts, which must hear all cases properly brought before them, the Supreme Court carefully chooses only the most important. Less than 2 percent of the some seven thousand petitions filed each year are granted. The Court did grant cert in *Lemon* and *DiCenso*, and both cases went on to the next step—briefing and oral arguments. The Court decided to handle these cases together. That might mean the Justices wanted to iron out conflicts between the lower court decisions or strike down one as a contrast to the other. The issues were just too much alike to treat the matters separately. The attorneys in the two states began to communicate with each other. In 1971, there were no fax machines or e-mail. Instead, the lawyers exchanged phone calls and letters.

Oral arguments take place in an impressive court-room of velvet and marble in Washington, D.C. The Justices share in a ritual handshake with each other as they all prepare to enter and take their seats at the bench. The procedure then is that each attorney has an allotted time to make arguments, but the Justices can interrupt with questions at any time, and they some-times do. The debate is often lively. The lawyers have to be ready to handle anything that the Justices want to ask and must walk up to the microphone with very broad knowledge of the law on the subject. The lawyers also must be prepared to handle "what if" questions about what effect their position, if adopted, will have on society. "I spent a sleepless night the night before, I can tell you," recalled Stanzler.[8] Afterward, he could not really tell how he had done.[9] Attorney Sawyer said, "We questioned whether any subject can be secular when taught in a Catholic school." As for his own views on religion, he says he's an agnostic. "If there's someone in charge, I don't know about it."[10] (An agnostic neither denies nor believes in the existence of God.)

The Court Deliberates

In the Supreme Court, Warren Burger as Chief Justice was in charge of this case. At conference, a private discussion among the Justices where even secretaries are not allowed, he led off by observing, "I don't see any difference between the Pennsylvania and Rhode Island plans," which met with agreement from everyone. "Entanglement is the only problem I see here," he continued, and that term indeed turned out to be a key word. He particularly noted, too, though, that "we have direct payments" to the religious institutions in both fact situations, which meant that an Establishment

Clause violation was likely.[11] Justice Harlan defended the schools, saying,

> If it's permissible, as I think it is, for public funds to be used for the "public school" part of religious schools and we can protect against trespass of religion into the public part, then policing is not entanglement in the sense of inhibiting recipients from using it for religion.[12]

Justice White took the most sympathetic view to the schools by far, claiming that "Entanglement is only another word for saying, as a matter of free exercise [of religious freedom] government can't muffle or inhibit one's religion."[13] Justices Douglas and Black were opposed, and Justice Blackmun warned, "Here are outright grants, which means the schools may use their own funds for other purposes. . . . The logical end to these . . . cases is complete support."[14] Justice Stewart complained, "Here the grants are beamed directly at helping the parochial schools."[15]

At the same time, they discussed a case that, under a federal law, gave one-time construction grants to sectarian (religious) colleges as long as the buildings were not to be used for religious worship or instruction. The case, *Tilton* v. *Richardson*, was eventually announced on the same day as *Lemon*.[16] The Chief Justice declared, "This can be distinguished from aid to

The *Tilton* v. *Richardson* case gave one-time construction grants to sectarian (religious) colleges as long as the buildings were not used for religious worship or instruction.

primary schools."[17] Younger children, he felt, were more impressionable and could not always tell that some government involvement intended no promotion of religion. But Justice Douglas identified what Justice Rehnquist later called a Catch-22 paradox—the government would need to closely monitor whether the buildings were being used properly. The way Justice Douglas put it was that "Unless the Government inspects to be sure, then [it is] not doing its duty and, if it does, then [there is] the entanglement that separation was intended to [prohibit]."[18] But even Justice Marshall, who usually was ready to find an Establishment Clause problem, expressed the belief that "Inspection is a normal governmental function and won't create improper intervention into religious institutions."[19]

The conference ended with an informal vote. In *Lemon* and *DiCenso*, Chief Justice Burger and Justices White, Marshall, and Harlan favored the private schools; Justices Black, Douglas, Stewart, and Blackmun opposed them. Justice Brennan wanted to see drafts of each opinion before committing himself. As for the federal case on colleges, seven Justices disagreed with Black and Douglas, who saw no real differences from the state cases and wanted all three state programs struck down.[20]

The next step was to assign the opinion to be written. But then Chief Justice Warren Burger received a call from Justice Brennan. Brennan had decided he was probably going to side with Burger. However, he said, he would rather not write the opinion. He told his aides that he hoped Burger would assign the task to Justice Harlan, who was known for restrained opinions, carefully written.[21]

The Chief Justice considered. He could assign cases to any Justice in the majority, though, like the other nine Justices, he had only one vote in arriving at that majority. He enjoyed the task of spreading out a large piece of butcher paper on his spacious desk, and tallying the names of the Justices and their cases. He was new to the Court. It was important to his image of leadership that he be in the majority most of the time. He would assign the writing of *Lemon* to the one he could trust the most—himself.[22]

4

Justice Burger and His Court

It was to be another glittering evening at the White House—a dinner in April 1969, at which "all the important Republicans" would be mingling.[1] Judge Warren E. Burger and his wife arrived early, and read the guest list. "If you get a feeling they're looking us over," he murmured to her, "act natural."[2] Burger *was*, in fact, being looked over. President Richard Nixon was looking for a new Chief Justice for the Supreme Court, and the solid, law-and-order record of Warren Burger appealed to him.

The next day, a colleague dropped by Burger's chambers, commenting that Burger had been the only judge at the dinner who was not on the Supreme

Court. "Looks like you're it," said appellate judge David Bazelon. Burger brushed that off. Another Justice, Potter Stewart, was seen as the most likely choice in the media.[3] But a week later, Stewart privately met with President Nixon and said that he was not willing to be elevated to the post. He did not want the publicity and pressure for himself and his family. It would also cause fewer hard feelings if a new person were brought in to lead rather than choosing one of the current members of the Court over another.[4]

Not long after, Democratic appointee Abe Fortas resigned his place on the bench as Republican president Nixon had hoped. Nixon then announced his choice of Warren Burger. Burger was astounded and honored. "A regular appointment [as a member of the Supreme Court] would have been enough. Chief was incredible."[5]

"The Counter-Revolution That Wasn't"

When Warren Burger laid his hand on a Bible and was sworn in as Chief Justice of the United States Supreme Court, many felt that the controversial Court rulings of the 1960s would be put to rest. Presidents Kennedy and Johnson had had their opportunities at posting like-minded people on the bench, and it was with "undisguised glee" that Nixon set about to change that.[6]

The previous Court, headed by Chief Justice Earl Warren, is generally agreed to have been an "activist" Court. It took upon itself new areas of law to decide, in favor of procedural rights for people accused of crime, equal housing and schooling access for African Americans, and free speech in questions of obscenity. Some historians say that the Court was unpopular at the time for its bold rulings forcing changes on American society.

Nixon wanted to curb the tendency of the Court in that direction. Opinion polls in 1968 said that Nixon was seen as someone who could address problems in the criminal justice system. For example, Warren Court decisions were seen as "soft" on criminals, and the crime rate was indeed rising. Some suspects had avoided jail time due to new Court rules on use of evidence and rights to free help from attorneys. Nixon had campaigned with promises to appoint Justices to the Supreme Court who would be tougher on criminals.[7] The late 1960s were a time of racial strife as well as protest over the war in Vietnam, and the decisions of the Court were only sparking more controversy. For example, Warren Court decisions barring prayer and Bible reading in school had sparked outrage in the public sector.[8]

But one scholar has called the Burger Court years

(1969–1986) "The Counter-Revolution that Wasn't."[9] Rather than overturning Warren Court precedents, Burger and the other Justices on the Court made "subtle, complicated changes," and in some cases even supported and extended the law that had been written in the Warren years.[10] For instance, the Burger Court's most famous decision, *Roe* v. *Wade*, which legalized abortion, was not popular with conservatives. Burger and the Justices who later joined him were cautious about discarding case precedent. They left a legacy that one author calls "neither liberal nor conservative."[11] They have even been criticized for their "lack of direction, at times even schizophrenia."[12] Burger himself would show a fondness for "balancing tests" that depended heavily on specific facts and the weighing of competing interests.[13] That approach would be demonstrated in *Lemon.*

Portrait of Warren Burger

Warren Burger was a "self-made man," according to most historians. He was the son of a traveling salesman, who helped his family in St. Paul, Minnesota, with odd jobs, and who worked his way through college.[14] He attended night school for his law degree, and then settled into a law practice where he handled contracts, real estate, and wills. During that time he became active

Lemon v. *Kurtzman* reached the Supreme Court in 1971. The nine Justices who presided over the case are shown here. Warren Burger (seated center) was the Chief Justice.

in state-level Republican politics, helping friends with their campaigns. As an appellate judge, he was known for his "jousts" with liberal attorneys.[15]

Burger attacked his duties as Chief Justice enthusiastically and improved many features of the Supreme Court facility. He found that secretaries and clerks were using old manual typewriters, and that the phone system was an old plug-in switchboard. He made plans to modernize these. He strolled through the building, asking that paint, landscaping, and the run-down cafeteria be updated. He noticed that the seating of the Justices for oral argument was in a straight line, making it hard for them to see each other and communicate. He proposed a curved bench and microphones to overcome the poor sound in the courtroom, so that all in the room could hear. And he decided to relocate the conference room where the Justices discussed cases to larger and more formal quarters, taking the lovely old paneled room with a chandelier for his own chambers.[16]

He energetically rethought the workload, procedures, and the place in society of the Supreme Court throughout his time in office. He spoke often about the role of the Supreme Court.[17] He "worked tirelessly to . . . reduce the friction between state and federal courts," and to encourage continuing education for judges. He also steered changes to juries, including reducing their size.[18] He once warned young people against becoming lawyers if they were trying to change the world. He said, "that is not the route by which basic changes in a country like ours should be made," and that they would face "some disappointments" if they tried.[19] Yet he liked to socialize with his young staff. He worked to make the Supreme Court more accessible to students and to the press.

The *Lemon* case would be one of the first ones he handled as Chief Justice. In that capacity, tradition required that he conduct discussion of each case, with each Justice speaking in order, beginning with the Justice with the least seniority. After general discussion—all done in privacy—he would assign the writing of the opinion to someone, or write it himself if he was part of the majority. Rough drafts of the opinion as well as disagreeing opinions, called dissents, would circulate for comments until a final form was favored by all.

One of the most important duties of the Chief Justice is to lead the others to a unanimous opinion if at all possible. This process helps the Court appear strong and makes the resulting law somewhat easier to understand and follow. Unfortunately, Chief Justice Burger was not very good at consensus building. It would be improper for the Justices to complain publicly about each other. Press leaks revealed, however, that Burger was not much liked as a leader.[20] Sometimes he would circulate his opinion drafts only to those Justices who already agreed with him, and then he would sometimes drop or drastically cut additions they suggested.[21] He spoke bluntly and seemed willing to pick a fight over ideas rather than bring all of the Justices together.[22]

The Justices

We will start with Justice Harry Blackmun, since he and Chief Justice Burger were often called "the Minnesota twins."[23] The two had been childhood friends, and Blackmun had been best man at Burger's wedding. But Blackmun had gone on to Harvard, and their paths had split. "[H]e [Blackmun] would explain how he had practiced in Minneapolis, where large law firms concentrated on serving major American corporations. . . . Burger had practiced in St. Paul, across the river, in the political, wheeler-dealer atmosphere of a state capital." Blackmun said, "A Minneapolis firm will never practice in St. Paul or vice versa."[24] Later, the two thought quite differently on cases, and Burger eventually assigned him the fewest cases during many terms—but at the time of the *Lemon* case, they voted together most of the time.[25]

Justice William Douglas

Justice William O. Douglas was a different sort of person. He had been on the Court for thirty years and showed that, as a humanist emphasizing the ultimate importance of people rather than God, he strongly desired limits on religion in the schools. He had been one of the "activist judges" who indulged "a willingness to create precedents" rather than follow tradition, and supported the "adjustment" of the Constitution "to the needs of time."[26] He was strong-willed, having faced conflict through his life. As a child he contracted polio and overcame it with the devoted care of his mother and determined exercise. Douglas's father died when Douglas was six, and the family had little money. He had lived in a tent for part of his early adult years and took odd jobs to get through college. He was a schoolteacher for two years before law school, and practiced and taught law before being appointed to the high Court as the youngest Justice in over one hundred years. He married four times, the last time to a college student almost fifty years his junior.[27] Before it became fashionable, he had a love of the outdoors and was an environmentalist.

Douglas wrote an unusual number of articles on law and politics. He had agreed to the Warren Court's removal of Bible reading and prayer by school officials.

Yet he was outspoken in favor of free speech. Chief Justice Burger would have to expect that if Douglas did not agree on the *Lemon* case, everyone would hear about it.[28]

Justice John Harlan

Justice John Marshall Harlan had a history of law in his respected family. His grandfather had served as an Associate Justice on the Court (1877–1911). The younger Harlan had been a good, though not outstanding, student, until he studied law and distinguished himself as first in his class at Oxford. He practiced law, and then served in the military in World War II. President Eisenhower appointed him to the Supreme Court in 1955. He was known for intellectual integrity, attention to detail, and balanced judgment. "[Law] students . . . freely acknowledge that when he has written a concurring or a dissenting opinion they read it first, for a full and candid exposition of the case and an intellectually rewarding analysis of the issues."[29] He had concurred with Burger in most religion cases or cases of which Burger approved, so he would probably join him again.

Justice William Brennan

Justice William J. Brennan was the only Catholic member of the Court at the time. He had attended public high school and then graduated from Harvard Law School. He had concurred in *Walz* v. *Tax Commission*, a case that upheld the tax-exempt status of church property as not violating the Establishment Clause.[30]

Yet he had written a colossal seventy-page concurrence in *Abington* v. *Schempp*, agreeing with the removal of school-led prayer in the public schools. This opinion, said one scholar, "still stands as one of the most powerful [statements in history] that a wall separating church and state should be not only maintained but also kept high."[31]

Chief Justice Burger recognized that Brennan was a powerful, persuasive coalition-builder on the Court. Justice Brennan had served on the Supreme Court of New Jersey. That court was an activist court (in favor of change) and was characterized by much the same kind of interactions to arrive at consensus that existed in the Warren Court.[32] He might be an opponent in the *Lemon* matter. If so, he would be a formidable one who would likely influence other Justices.

Justice Byron White

Justice Byron White was a member of the bench who had a more conservative (traditional) point of view. He had the Protestant work ethic that matched Burger's

The Supreme Court building in Washington, D.C., where the Justices ruled on the *Lemon* case is shown here.

own. As White recalled of his childhood, "by the normal standards of today we were all quite poor, although we didn't necessarily know it because everyone was more or less the same. Everybody worked for a living. Everybody. Everybody." White was especially influenced by his older brother and won the same two scholarships his brother had. He was nicknamed "Whizzer" for his rushing career in football and was named to the collegiate Hall of Fame in 1954. He had progressed from there to clerking for a Supreme Court Justice. The clerking position was an important job, since clerks often have a significant impact on the decisions written, and sometimes are the main authors of them.[33] Warren Burger probably counted him as an ally in the *Lemon* case, but that would turn out to be only partially true.

Justice Potter Stewart

Justice White and Justice Potter Stewart were considered "centrists" who might be a "swing vote" either way on a particular issue. They did not hold predictable positions. But Justice Stewart was a bit more polished and sophisticated. His writing was clear, his thinking was fair and cautious, and his philosophy was hard to imitate.[34] He had written a dissent in *Abington v. Schempp*. He pointed out that the free exercise rights of religious parents to have their child's school day open with prayer was being denied by outlawing those prayers in the public schools.[35] And he had joined in Burger's opinion in the *Walz* case. But he liked to draw distinctions based on specific facts and was honest about it. He did not take himself too seriously. In recalling his military career in the Navy during World War II, he said he had spent the time "Floating around on a sea of 100-octane gas, bored to death 99 percent of the time and scared to death 1 percent."[36]

Justice Thurgood Marshall

Justice Thurgood Marshall was the first African-American member of the Supreme Court. Marshall's great-grandfather had been a slave. Young Thurgood grew up in Baltimore, Maryland, and he

> had ample opportunity to learn the United States Constitution by heart at an early age. He tended to be unruly in elementary school, and for punishment on numerous occasions the principal sent him to the basement to memorize a section of the document.[37]

He was rejected from one law school on the basis of race, but distinguished himself elsewhere. He later began a distinguished career with the National Association for the Advancement of Colored People (NAACP).[38] He often argued cases before the Supreme

Court to which President Lyndon Johnson eventually appointed him. "His social perception was that life represents a never-ending struggle between the advantaged and disadvantaged . . . [and] that legal activism is both a valued and imperative tool in helping the disadvantaged in that struggle."[39] He usually found Establishment Clause violations where they were at issue. Justice Burger would have to look elsewhere for a vote upholding the funding in *Lemon*.

Justice Hugo Black

Justice Hugo Black was born in a log cabin in 1886. He had been on the bench quite awhile by the time Chief Justice Warren Burger arrived. Justice Black had given his opinion on Establishment Clause issues before. In one case that held that public school districts could lend textbooks free to private schools, Black dissented (disagreed). He said,

> This links state and churches together in controlling the lives and destinies of our citizenship—a citizenship composed of people of myriad religious faiths, some of them bitterly hostile to and completely intolerant of the others.[40]

In deciding that taxes could not be given to religious schools to bus students, he said, "the clause against establishment of religion by law was intended to erect 'a wall of separation between church and State.'"[41] The phrase "separation of church and state" does not appear in the Constitution, however. And Black cited no authority for the statement. Decades of history had seen public funds used for even more purely religious functions, such as maintaining chaplains for Congress and the military. Black had signaled how he would be inclined to rule in *Lemon*.

Justice Black was called a combination of "the steel hard and the soft." He would often succeed in changing the other Justices' views on a case with a variety of polite but pointed legal memos. His manner was that of a gracious southerner.[42]

This was the combination of experience and viewpoints that the Court brought to the *Lemon* case. How they would combine to form a decision remained to be seen.

5

The Ruling

As Chief Justice Warren Burger began to write the opinions on *Lemon, DiCenso,* and *Tilton,* he had to respond primarily to two things: precedent, or the case law already created by the Court, and the briefs, or written arguments by attorneys. In addition, the Justices could consider the *amicus* briefs. *Amicus curiae* is Latin for "friend of the court." It means that a person or organization, not actually involved in the case, that has some expertise and interest in the issues of the case, is allowed by the Court to file written arguments, or briefs, about the case. In this case, over thirty such briefs had been filed, an indication of a high degree of public interest. *Amici* briefs included various Jewish and other religious organizations, state attorneys general, and school administrators.

Roots of the *Lemon* Test

Besides briefs, three precedents in particular would have to be addressed. First, in *Board of Education* v. *Allen*, decided before Chief Justice Burger came to the Court, the Justices had held that loaning textbooks to private schools was not a First Amendment violation. They had used the "child-benefit analysis" reasoning that the government money went to children and their parents and did not directly benefit religion. By contrast, another case had rejected funding for bus service to a private school because the money did not go to families, but directly to the religious schools.[1]

Second, in *Walz* v. *Tax Commission*, the Court had examined the question of tax exempt status for the property belonging to churches. (Cities and other state agents usually are able to collect taxes from property owners. Churches have never paid these taxes because they have been historically exempt.) In upholding the exemption, the Chief Justice had used much of the analysis Justice Brennan had suggested. He emphasized history and the fact that religious organizations contribute to America's diversity of ideas.[2] Chief Justice Burger would have to show how the present cases were different. He wrote that there was no historical precedent in the United States for public support of religious instruction. It would be impossible to separate the religious functions of the schools from the secular.[3] He noted that the school programs in question were innovative, not traditional. On the other hand, he stated, there was a two-hundred-year history of property tax exemptions.[4]

He then reviewed the standards that the Court had used in *Walz* and previous cases for determining if there had been a violation of the Establishment Clause. From *Board of Education* v. *Allen,* he relied on these two criteria: Whether the state law or activity has a *secular purpose,* and whether its principal or *primary effect* is to advance or inhibit religion. He ignored the child-benefit analysis. From *Walz,* he took the third factor: that an *excessive government entanglement* with religion must not be allowed.[5] Together these factors became the three-pronged *Lemon* test.

The attorney for Alton Lemon, Henry W. Sawyer III, urged the three-pronged test in his brief, and said, "I claim credit for that. I created the three-prong test." He recalled that he based it heavily on James Madison's essay "Memorial and Remonstrance," which emphasized that "you can't have interdependence between church and state."[6] Madison's work is again quoted heavily in *Lemon*. It appears mostly in Justice Douglas's concurrence, or agreeing opinion, not in Burger's main opinion.[7]

Ironing Out the Differences

Entanglement turned out to be the key problem in the
Lemon case. Yet it was Justice Brennan's draft of the
Walz opinion, not Chief Justice Burger's, that initially
targeted it. Justice Brennan had called the issue
"extensive state involvement with religion." Chief
Justice Burger made it more concrete by renaming it
"excessive government entanglement with religion."[8]
On May 25, 1971, he talked with Justice Brennan more
about *Tilton,* the companion case to *Lemon.* Tilton
allowed federal money to build campus structures on
religious college property. There was a twenty-year limit
on using the buildings for only secular purposes. Chief
Justice Burger thought that Justice Brennan might agree
with him if they decided to strike down the limit,
meaning that the buildings could never be used for
religion. But by then, Justice Brennan had decided to
write his own concurrence in *Lemon* and *DiCenso,* and
vote against the *Tilton* funding entirely.[9] Justice
Brennan had lunch with Justice Harlan several days
later and urged striking down all three funding
arrangements. Justice Harlan showed interest in that
but later the same day told the other Justices that he had
decided to vote with Chief Justice Burger.[10] Justice
Blackmun joined two days later. Justice Marshall was
still deciding. He had been part of a "bloc," or

consistent voting pattern, with Justices Douglas and Brennan, but here those two were split.[11] In this case, Justice Marshall joined Justice Douglas in both the state and federal cases, though for unstated reasons, he did not actually join in either side on *DiCenso*.[12]

Everyone had spoken. Justice White concurred in *DiCenso* and *Tilton* but dissented in *Lemon*.[13] Although Chief Justice Burger had a clear majority, he began the opinion with some humility, saying that "we can only dimly perceive the lines of demarcation in this extraordinarily sensitive area of constitutional law."[14] He then discussed each prong of the test in application to the facts.

First, he said that the funding laws in question had a secular purpose. A secular purpose is one that is meaningful to the whole community, not just to religious persons. Examples of a secular purpose would include promoting health, reducing crime, or, here, assisting education.

> [T]he statutes themselves clearly state that they are intended to enhance the quality of the secular education in all schools covered by the compulsory [mandatory] attendance laws. There is no reason to believe the legislatures [lawmakers] meant anything else.[15]

It is easy to see why it is in society's interest to educate children. Here, providing books or teachers is the kind of secular purpose allowable.

Students pray with teachers at a private school in Oklahoma. Private religious schools cannot receive government funding.

Next, the Chief Justice declined to apply the "primary effect of advancing religion" prong, explaining that this one was not necessary because the next prong, entanglement, was clearly violated.[16] Actually this sort of sidestepping of questions is fairly common. It is traditional for courts to rule no farther than is necessary to resolve a case. And so, the Chief Justice went on to discuss entanglement.

He observed that

> Our prior holdings do not call for total separation between church and state. . . . Fire inspections [of churches and church schools, and], building and zoning regulations are examples of necessary and permissible contacts.[17]

He cited prior cases that allowed bus transportation, school lunches, health services, and textbooks for parochial (religious) schools.[18] He pointed out that a textbook's appropriateness can be decided one time for everyone. It is impossible, however, to monitor teachers closely to make sure their secular and religious functions remain separated.[19] He also noted that a bishop and a priest had oversight over the hiring and contract negotiations for the schools. In addition, the states had to audit the books of the schools to make sure they spent money only on secular topics, entangling the church with the state even further.[20]

The next section of the opinion contained a crucial point. Chief Justice Warren Burger had identified "political divisiveness," or splitting a community, as another danger to the Establishment Clause. He said that offering money to private schools would create political scrambling for the funds, giving rise to "political division along religious lines." This was "one of the principal evils against which the First Amendment was intended to protect."[21] He cited no authority about the Founding Fathers' intent at all for this point, however. He cited only cases that had been written in the last twenty years—cases that documented nothing from history. Perhaps because politics was the most difficult factor to defend, he did not make it a fourth prong in the *Lemon* test. He simply used it to support the outcome.[22]

He concluded his reasoning in *Lemon* with the following: "[W]hile some involvement and entanglement are inevitable, lines must be drawn."[23] The lines were drawn, and the cases remanded, or sent back, to their original courts for any further proceedings.

Those Who Concurred—Different Paths to the Same Finish

The Burger opinion did not suit some of the Justices perfectly. Justice Douglas filed a concurrence (agreeing opinion) to include all the language he desired in the opinion. This sometimes is done when a Justice agrees with the result in a majority opinion but wants to add some additional reasoning to support it. Douglas said that "The tax payers have a voice in the way their money is used in the public school, but the people who support a parochial school have no voice at all in such affairs."[24] This argument might come as a surprise to many people who are forced on threat of imprisonment to pay taxes regardless of their opinion of the schools. It might also surprise parents and donors to private schools, who can withdraw their tuition or support at any time. Justice Douglas also said that the purpose of religious schools (he specified Catholic schools) "is not so much to educate, but to indoctrinate and train, not to teach . . . but to make Roman Catholics. . . ."[25]

Justice Brennan also wanted his own approach kept separate. His concurrence was almost twenty pages long. He wanted his to cover *Tilton* also. He saw no difference between the federal and state funding plan.[26] It is interesting to note that he turned back to a three-part test, but it was not Chief Justice Burger's. He quoted from concurrences in *Abington* v. *Schempp* and *Walz*, saying that

What the Framers meant to foreclose [prevent], and what our decisions under the Establishment Clause have forbidden, are those involvements of religious with secular institutions which (a) serve the essentially religious activities of religious institutions; (b) employ the organs of government for essentially religious purposes; or (c) use essentially religious means to serve governmental ends, where secular means would suffice.[27]

Unfortunately for Justice Brennan, this additional set of criteria has not attracted a following. It is impossible to use both tests unless we want to add to the check-off list endlessly. Eventually, by some criterion, anything could offend the Establishment Clause. The test must be simple and concrete enough for people to understand and use to govern their conduct.

Justice Brennan's opinion traced the history of government support for private schools, citing several examples of it. "[G]overnment generally looked to the church to provide education, and often contributed support through donations of land and money."[28] For instance, he said, in 1786 " . . . the first New York legislature [lawmakers] ordered that one section in each township be set aside for the 'gospel and schools.'"[29] But he said that as time went by, "[t]he Nation's rapidly developing religious heterogeneity [diversity], the tide of . . . democracy, and growing urbanization soon led to

70

widespread demands throughout the States for secular public education."[30] He said public funds could now only be contributed to religious schools in very limited ways.

One last opinion emerged. Justice White concurred in *Lemon* and *Tilton*, but could not agree with *DiCenso*. In other words, he believed all three funding plans were constitutional. He began by reminding us that, "The States are not only permitted, but required by the Constitution, to free students attending private schools from any public school attendance obligation."[31] He took issue with Justice Douglas's comment that religious schools did not care about mastery of secular knowledge, saying instead that ". . . good secular instruction is . . . essential to the success of the religious mission of the parochial school."[32] Justice White finished by saying he saw no legal difference among the programs. The Court's admission that the line separating church and state is "blurred, indistinct, and variable," should have been a signal to resolve all doubts in favor of the free-exercise-of-religion in private schools.[33] He did use Chief Justice Burger's test. He felt, however, that the school's freedom to exercise its religion outweighed some entanglement concerns.[34]

New Input on the Court

Two years went by, and two of the Justices left the bench. Justice Black died, and Justice Harlan retired. They were replaced with two attorneys. One of them would eventually rise to the position of the next Chief Justice.

Justice Lewis Powell was already sixty-four years old when he was appointed. He brought excellent credentials of nonpolitical service—he had been president of the American Bar Association and of the American College of Trial Lawyers. He was widely acclaimed for his compassion and sense of fairness. Possibly he could supply some help in striking compromises, since he was known to be a good mediator. "Powell seemed ideally suited to exert a calming influence" on the Court.[35] As the ancestor of one of the original Jamestown settlers in America, he might be expected to be sensitive to the Founding Fathers' inclusion of religious elements in the public schools. On the other hand, he had also been chairman of the Richmond Public School Board and the State Board of Education. He might see taxpayer funding of private materials as a drain on the public schools.

Justice William Rehnquist, then a vigorous new member of the Court, was Chief Justice Warren Burger's other new colleague. He had seemed to be Richard Nixon's ideal jurist, whom the president expected to [interpret] the Bill of Rights . . . "strictly" to reverse the Warren Court's [previous] expansion of protections for criminal defendants and, in general, to favor a more modest role for the Court.[36]

Young William Rehnquist was raised in a strongly Republican household. When asked by his elementary-school teacher about his career hopes, Rehnquist said, "I'm going to change the government."[37] He graduated from Stanford Law School first in his class. (Sandra Day, his classmate, later to be Supreme Court Justice Sandra Day O'Connor, finished third.) One of his duties at the Justice Department later was to screen candidates for potential Supreme Court positions. In replacing retiring Justice Harlan, the attorney general gave Rehnquist the news that someone had been chosen—Rehnquist himself. His written opinions were known as "passionate, eminently . . . logical, dramatic, sarcastic, [and] powerful," and some said he was "the best mind on the Court."[38] He also secured an additional place in history when he presided over the impeachment trial of President Bill Clinton.

Lemon II

The battle of *Lemon I* as it is now known, was not over. The winners in *Lemon I* felt that any government payment to a religious school was illegal. They went back to court to enjoin, or stop, the payment of any money to the private schools that had been made during the time the case had been before the courts. This conflict illustrates the very common problem of whether or not a court decision should be retroactive. That is, should the parties involved have to go back and undo everything that had been done when the Court had found that the situation was unconstitutional? Here, the teachers being paid could not go back and "unteach" the schoolchildren. Sometimes court rulings, Justice Burger wrote, "are a special blend of what is necessary, what is fair, and what is workable."[39] Here, the Court just did not like the idea of taking money away from teachers and librarians who had already worked for children by making *Lemon I* apply to past situations. So they limited the effect of their ruling to the future.

Some of the Justices disagreed. In a dissent, Justices Douglas, Brennan, and Stewart said that, "There is as much a violation of the Establishment Clause of the First Amendment whether the payment from school funds to sectarian schools involves last year, the current year, or next year."[40] The majority, however, felt that anything harmful to the Constitution had already been done. Only a onetime accounting for purposes of "cleanup" remained. The problem had arisen "only once under special circumstances that will not recur," they assured the rest.[41]

Thus concluded the case that had resulted in a flurry of judicial opinions. What would remain after the dust settled? What would reactions be to this decision? How would those reactions affect future decisions?

6

The Impact of the Case

Reaction to the *Lemon* decision was minimal. The limited reaction might be because many states did not have funding plans like those in *Lemon*, and were unaffected. Or perhaps it was because the announcement of the test simply satisfied people who wanted guidelines for the future. Maybe it was due to the fact that the three-pronged test was really not new, but was pieced together from existing cases. In addition, so many other Supreme Court decisions were more controversial, that this one might have seemed relatively acceptable. Or perhaps the announcement of the test made the case too complicated for the average person to digest. For example, the attorney, Henry Sawyer, who worked on both *Lemon* and *Abington* v. *Schempp*, said of *Schempp*, on school prayer, it "created much greater emotion—because it's easier to understand."[1]

Whatever the reason, Chief Justice Warren Burger must have been pleased that there was not much negative reaction in the press. He wanted to begin a new era for the Supreme Court, one during which the Court was more accepted by the public because its rulings were more in tune with mainstream America. One historian said that by the time the previous Chief left the bench, ". . . the Supreme Court had reached its nadir [low point] in public esteem."[2] In 1971, the year this decision was announced, a Harris poll indicated that only 23 percent of those polled indicated that they had "a great deal of confidence in . . . the people running the U.S. Supreme Court," and Establishment Clause rulings had contributed to that erosion of confidence.[3]

Though the decision may not have sparked intense reaction, it has powerfully influenced the law. While the more visible *Abington* has been cited in later cases over one thousand times, *Lemon* has been cited over twenty-two hundred times. It has, however, received mixed reviews. One scholar has complained that "the test has had little restraining power on the Court." The three-pronged test is almost an invitation to judges to scrutinize many situations for suspected violations of the Establishment Clause.[4] It has also been criticized as too easily made to serve preplanned results. According to another scholar, there is "no evidence that such a test actually guides the Court in reaching a decision that would not have been reached without it."[5] Using the same test, one critic claims, people can "often arrive at contradictory results."[6]

One law professor refers to *Lemon* as an example of "The Burger Court's addiction to uneasy, middle-of-the-road doctrines."[7] In other words, he sensed a tendency in the Court to write opinions that made compromises to satisfy the two parties in the case but did not establish solid principles to use widely. He listed a number of such decisions about funding of religious schools, starting with Lemon, that "summarize the middle course [full of] numerous fine, unconvincing distinctions."[8]

States are *not* permitted to

- help pay teachers in sectarian elementary and secondary schools;
- contribute to maintaining religious schools' facilities;
- help such schools finance field trips to public facilities;

- lend those schools maps, charts, films, and instructional equipment; or

- reimburse the parents of religious school students for tuition expenses.

However, states *are* permitted to

- finance the construction of buildings devoted solely to secular purposes on sectarian college campuses;

- lend secular textbooks to students in religious schools; and

- underwrite a portion of the general operating expenses of religious colleges.[9]

Endless variations in facts account for the apparently inconsistent rulings. But the fact-sensitive nature of the *Lemon* test can keep us careful to avoid establishments of religion. It is important to note that the Court could have simply ruled on the facts of *Lemon* and *DiCenso* without clarifying criteria for deciding future situations. But one scholar has said that when Chief Justice Burger came onto the Court, the "challenge" of spelling out some kind of standard of church and state "was the principal issue of Establishment Clause law."[10] Burger's test was the

Court's attempt to meet that challenge. To review, the test requires the following three things:

1. The law must have a secular (nonreligious) purpose.

2. Its principal or primary effect must be one that neither advances nor inhibits religion.

3. The law must not promote "an excessive government entanglement with religion."[11]

All these prongs are very fact-sensitive and call for practicality. The test, particularly the entanglement prong, is, as Chief Justice Burger said in the *Walz* case,

> inescapably one of degree. Either course, taxation of churches or exemption, occasions some degree of involvement with religion. Elimination of exemption would tend to expand the involvement of government by giving rise to tax valuation of church property, tax foreclosures, and the direct confrontations and conflicts that follow in the train of those legal procedures.[12]

This kind of nuts-and-bolts approach to the Chief Justice's decisions may account for the durability of the *Lemon* test.

Although he set the course for the Court and the country with *Lemon*, Chief Justice Burger wrote only two other majority opinions on the Establishment Clause. Both came out some ten years after *Lemon*.

Larkin v. *Grendel's Den, Inc.* struck down a state law that allowed churches to veto applications for the issuance of liquor licenses within five hundred feet of a church.[13] Burger opened the conference discussion by saying, "The statute is invalid on its face in delegating power to a private party. . . . [It's] not important that it's a church. But the fact that it's a church makes it easier. . . ." He added that under the law there did not even seem to be any "review power over the church's decision, as I see it," so that the church had a complete veto over what businesses located in the area.[14]

Justice White agreed, though he said that a flat ban on any alcohol sale within a given distance, without letting churches veto certain businesses, would be constitutional. Justice Rehnquist voted for the law, but the others on the Court agreed with Chief Justice Burger to strike it down—except, that is, for the new member of the Court, Sandra Day O'Connor, who just said, "On the Establishment Clause, I'm not at rest, so I will pass."[15] The other majority opinion Chief Justice Burger authored on this subject was *Lynch* v. *Donnelly*.[16] In this case, the plaintiff brought a suit complaining that a crèche (figures depicting the birth of Christ in a stable) was placed by a city in a public place at public expense. This display, it was argued, offended the Establishment Clause. The Chief Justice

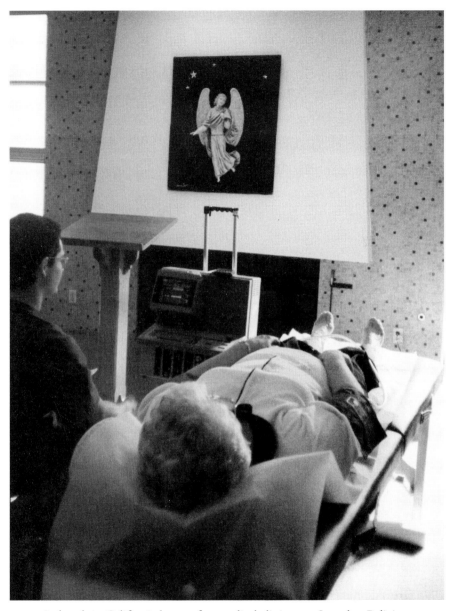

A church in California hosts a free medical clinic on a Saturday. Religious organizations can receive government funding if the money serves a secular need such as this one.

disagreed in conference. "This has been a practice for over a century. . . . Whether it's part of a larger scene or separate, I see no First Amendment violation. It's not a secular activity, but it's no different from chaplains for me." (Here he was referring to *Marsh* v. *Chambers*, the decision allowing state lawmakers to pay a member of the clergy to open each day with a prayer.)[17] "This would pass the [*Lemon* v.] *Kurtzman* tests."[18]

Justice Marshall protested the purely cultural and historical arguments favoring the crèche. "Christ is not like a Thanksgiving turkey."[19] Justice Brennan, too, later noted that to treat the display as

> no different from Santa's house or reindeer is not only offensive to those for whom the creche has profound significance, but insulting to those who insist for religious or personal reasons that the story of Christ is in no sense a part of "history" nor an unavoidable element of our national heritage.[20]

Justices Rehnquist and Blackmun were inclined to ignore the whole topic. Rehnquist called the objection to the crèche a "peewee." "People are not really bothered by this in its Christmas context."[21] Justice Blackmun concluded, ". . . [P]ublic support leads me to affirm."[22] Most of the Justices agreed that *Marsh* did not shed light on this situation, and they allowed the crèche to stand. Chief Justice Burger avoided the secular purpose prong by saying that the secular purpose of the display was to celebrate a holiday, not promote a religion.[23] Justice O'Connor filed a concurrence that treated the scene as a dialogue, with the state being the speaker and the passersby being the hearers.

> The purpose prong asks whether government's actual purpose is to endorse or disapprove of religion. The effect prong asks whether, irrespective of government's actual purpose, the practice under review in fact conveys a message of endorsement.[24]

Entanglement was not an important issue. Justice O'Connor concluded that the government's intent was not to promote religion but to participate in the culture. The reasonable observer would not mistake the display for support of religion.[25]

Application of the *Lemon* test in school cases continued to be applied to other fact situations with various results. Overall we can identify four important trends in Establishment Clause cases.

Trends in the Law Since *Lemon*

First, the Court seems to be favoring practicality in letting children be educated over abstract concerns about Establishment Clause violations. For example, in

Aguilar v. *Felton*, a state program that allowed public-school teachers to go into religious schools to give help to disadvantaged children, was struck down in 1985. Under Presidents Reagan and Bush, the Elementary and Secondary Education Act of 1965 was sometimes used to allow this.[26] The Court found that doing so violated the Establishment Clause. The Court assumed teachers were going to teach some religious ideas at the religious schools.[27] As a result, New York City spent millions of dollars to pay for trailers to be used for that purpose. Yet in 1997, with *Agostini* v. *Felton*, the Court again addressed the issue. This time the court reversed *Aguilar* and held that educating religious handicapped children was in the best interest of society—that is, it was a legitimate secular purpose. There was no automatic Establishment Clause violation when public funds were used to pay teachers who helped out in religious schools. The Court said we do not have to assume that if publicly funded teachers work on a private school campus, that they will begin to teach religion.[28]

Another trend that has emerged since *Lemon* is that of allowing students more expression of their religious beliefs and school officials a bit less. Through the Department of Education, President Bill Clinton sent guidelines in 1995 concerning religion in the public schools to every school superintendent in the country. One 1995 headline in *USA Today* summarized the guidelines this way: "Students can express views [on religion]; schools can't."[29] In the case of *Lee* v. *Weisman* a school worked with a local rabbi to prepare a prayer for a middle school graduation. The Court found an establishment of religion. It based its finding on the entanglement of the school with editing and monitoring religious expression, and then appearing to endorse it from the podium.[30]

On the other hand, student expression and prayer in the same situation have been upheld, though student graduation prayer has yet to be decided on by the Supreme Court.[31]

The so-called forum analysis is an important development in the law as well. Forum analysis is analysis of speech according to where the speech takes place. While Warren Burger was Chief Justice, the Court basically looked at whether public or private money was spent on the religious expression. Since then, the question has been more focused on whether a forum has been opened for discussion on a given topic. If so, any public officials involved cannot censor, or block out, a religious message. In *Lamb's Chapel* v. *Center Moriches*, the Rehnquist Court unanimously held that when a public school opened its campus to groups to discuss community and cultural affairs, it had opened a forum. It, therefore, could not refuse to rent to a religious group that wanted to show a film on a subject from an explicitly religious viewpoint.[32]

In a related Rehnquist Court case, a student at the University of Virginia sued the state school because student activity fees were used for some student publications and not his religious one. He won, with the Court saying that a religious viewpoint cannot be the object of discrimination by a public institution.[33]

A fourth trend we can observe is the distinction made between establishing a religion and allowing religious principles and people into public discussions. For instance, no secular purpose was found for posting the Ten Commandments in a public school. The Court let stand, however, a lower court ruling that a company could require its employees to learn a number of moral principles based on Bible passages.[34] That practice was found to be justified by the legitimate, secular purpose of enhancing ethics and morale at the company.[35]

Does the *Lemon* Test Still Apply?

Since *Lemon* was handed down, the three-pronged test has been applied to many situations. However, the Court has also added more things to look for in identifying an establishment of religion, and sometimes even ignores the *Lemon* test.

- One later case simply asked if the funds used for religious schools were made available to both religious and secular schools in a neutral fashion by neutral criteria.[36]

- Other cases have asked whether it appeared to a reasonable observer that the state was endorsing religion. Justice O'Connor has frequently used this approach.[37]

- Still others find an establishment of religion if the activity would be divisive, or bitterly controversial, in the community.[38]

- Another case examined the motives of the public officials who had passed a law against a controversial voodoo practice. The Court struck down the law because the officials openly stated that their motive, or desire, was to stamp out animal sacrifice.[39] In such cases, the practice is protected under the equal protection guarantee in the Fourteenth Amendment.

- Elsewhere a religious practice in a government

A county courthouse in New Mexico displays the Ten Commandments. The monument was donated and is maintained by a private group. The Supreme Court has ruled, however, that there is no secular purpose for posting the Ten Commandments in a public school.

setting has prevailed because it was a historical exception. The Court made such an exception, in *Marsh* v. *Chambers*, for the practice of lawmakers opening sessions with prayer.[40]

These are only some of the criteria that have been used to decide these cases. This variety of standards is unusual in the law, and can be confusing. Until the case law becomes more uniform, people do not know when an establishment of religion might be found, partly because they do not even know what set of rules controls the situation. Indeed, they will probably not know until a lawsuit is filed and an opinion rendered. One Supreme Court Justice has complained that

> The secret of the *Lemon* test's survival, I think, is that it is so easy to kill. It is there to scare us [and our audience] when we wish it to do so, but we can command it to return to the tomb at will. . . . When we wish to strike down a practice it forbids, we invoke it, . . . when we wish to uphold a practice it forbids, we ignore it entirely. . . . Sometimes, we take a middle course, calling its three prongs 'no more than helpful signposts. . . .'[41]

Patterns do seem to emerge about when the *Lemon* test is used and when other guidelines are followed. Currently it appears that the Supreme Court first looks for the following:

- any obvious verbal statement by a government official that is claimed to be an establishment of religion, as in the voodoo case;[42]

- cases where the issue is whether taxes are funding religious activities. In these cases the *Lemon* test is applied. Often, the recent Justices look to whether there is not just entanglement but excessive entanglement between church and state. *Some* entanglement between the two cannot be avoided and is not constitutionally fatal.[43]

The Court uses the "endorsement" test in ceremonial and display cases (where the issue is whether the government appears to be making a statement). An instance of this occurs when a city puts on a holiday display and risks appearing to endorse, or promote, a religious holiday.[44] If the controversy is about free speech, the forum analysis is the basis for deciding the case. Thus, the Court has held that if a state university has opened up a forum for speech by spending student activity fees for student publications, religious publications can be funded along with nonreligious ones.[45]

In *Agostini* v. *Felton*, the Court decided that entanglement (third prong) of the government with the church is really an effect (second prong). That is, the Court assumes that entangling religion and government will promote religion. While many religious people would dispute that, we can now refer to the "two-prong *Lemon* test" instead of the three-prong one. A federal court recently explained the new *Lemon* test this way: [t]he post-*Agostini Lemon* test included the first (secular purpose) prong plus the following, re-tooled "effect prong":

> . . . whether government aid has the effect of advocating religion; [does the aid] result in governmental indoctrination; [does the aid] define its recipients by reference to religion; or [does the aid] create an excessive entanglement[?][46]

Again, this set of standards shows the Court's increasing practicality. It looks to what results, or what is created, as well as the intentions of those involved, which are all matters of facts and evidence, rather than abstract legal rules.

Lemon has been added to, condensed, sometimes ignored, and sometimes changed; nevertheless, its usefulness remains. Just when one commentator might think it is out of date, it appears in another ruling. Supreme Court Justice Antonin Scalia said this of the *Lemon* test:

[L]ike some ghoul in a late-night horror movie that repeatedly sits up in its grave and shuffles abroad. . . . *Lemon* stalks our Establishment Clause jurisprudence once again, frightening the little children and school attorneys. . . .[47]

He noted that ". . . no fewer than five of the currently sitting Justices have, in their own opinions, personally driven pencils through the creature's heart. . .," but Scalia went on to say that *Lemon* is a "useful monster. . . worth keeping around. . . . One never knows when one might need him."[48] His colleagues on the Court answered,

While we are somewhat diverted [amused] by Justice Scalia's evening at the cinema, . . . we return to the reality that there is a proper way to inter [bury] an established decision, and *Lemon*, however frightening it might be to some, has not been overruled.[49]

In the next chapter we will discuss other, more recent, ideas about the relationship of government to religion.

7

Beyond Lemon

Hillsdale College is an institution that has never accepted any government funds. One official of the college has a favorite saying: "Whom the gods would destroy, they first subsidize."[1] When a powerful entity, like the government, wants to take control over something such as business or a college, it can do so by starting to give it money. Gradually the recipient of the money becomes dependent on the money and starts being influenced by the strings attached to the money. As one principal of a private school says, "I don't want government aid. I don't want an 800-pound gorilla to fall in love with me."[2]

These statements point to the dangers, usually unintended, of government ties to institutions such as churches. But other people recognize the dangers to government as well. In discussing a law that required businesses to be closed on Sunday, the Christian Sabbath, scholar Robert Cord warned,

> This is one of the odious incidentals that characterized established religions in Europe, accepted legal discrimination against individuals whose religious faith was allegedly aided. . . . [by this type of law].[3]

We can observe the problems in our day with situations such as that in China. All Christians there are required to register with the government's official church. Those who do not are harassed or tortured. In Sudan, women are required to cover all exposed skin when dressing, in accordance with Muslim tradition. Women who resist face imprisonment or the threat of being sold into slavery.[4]

In the United States, our Constitution guarantees us the "free exercise of religion." The law requires government to accommodate our religions, or lack of them, and to avoid "inhibiting religion." Government is also finding that faith-based institutions are more cost-effective than government programs at things like drug treatment programs.[5] Poor and minority students in religious schools are four times more likely to graduate, and three times more likely to go to college, than those in public schools.[6] Church-related day care centers and school programs show success and usually operate on a limited budget.[7] A religious outreach to teens called "The Spot" was effectively motivating kids to turn away from drugs and crime in one city. City officials turned down a request for grant money; but four years later, they came to The Spot "with one question: Why is the church's idea for a youth center working and the city's isn't? [The leader] told them that the power and presence of Christ made the difference."[8]

There has been some concern about religious centers that accept tax dollars and also share their faith. Sometimes questions arise about matters such as whether children at a federally funded day care programs can say grace before eating their snack, or whether a mental hospital can counsel patients in matters of faith. For example, a nursing home in Arizona was sued for showing a religious film, although many residents wanted it shown. The accusation was that the tax support of the home meant tax support for the message of the film. The Supreme Court rejected this reasoning. It held that the film was not an establishment of religion, but a recognition of free speech in an open forum.[9] According to one survey, 68 percent of Americans want tax money to flow toward some of these proven religious programs. However, the institutions are going to have to be vigilant to make sure that they do not become dependent on that tax money.[10]

Alternatives to traditional tax-funded education are springing up around the country. Vouchers, charter schools, home schooling, and released time are some of these alternatives. A voucher is a check from the government that a parent can put toward expenses of alternative schooling. In November 1998, the Supreme Court let stand a Wisconsin ruling upholding the validity of a voucher program. It found that the system did not promote an establishment of religion. Under the system in question, sixty-two hundred low-income students were allowed forty-nine hundred dollars each to attend about ninety different private schools in Milwaukee, Wisconsin.[11] We are safe in assuming that Chief Justice Burger would have approved. He said of several cases, including *Lemon*, "The essence of all these decisions, I suggest, is that government aid to individuals generally stands on an entirely different footing from direct aid to religious institutions."[12]

Charter schools are public schools funded with taxes, but they are run by a private company under a contract with the state. They are intended to have more freedom from regulations imposed on regular schools. The money involved cannot be used to promote religion in a charter school, but religious institutions

98

Oklahoma congressman Steve Largent was chairperson of the National Prayer Breakfast in 1999. The Congressional Prayer Breakfast has been sponsored by members of Congress in their private capacities since 1952.

can form separate corporations to run schools and hold worship services outside of school hours. In 1998, public school parents in one Georgia high school voted 98 percent in favor of becoming a charter. One hundred new charter schools were offered in the state of New York for fall 1999 and were received enthusiastically among parents.[13]

Another wave of the future in education is home schooling. All fifty states allow it, and home-schooled students have no more trouble getting into colleges and universities than public school students.[14] It is a movement that is on the rise. About 1.5 million children now go to school in their living room or at the kitchen table.[15] These families pay taxes for the public schools and pay again to educate their own children by purchasing curriculum, supplies, enrichment coaching, and laboratory equipment, as well as staying home from other work to teach. Families of private school students pay their taxes and also pay private school tuition. Rather than try to avoid their taxes, some families and lawmakers have begun to think about how taxes could help them in their own efforts to educate their kids. One constitutional scholar puts it this way, "That some parents wish their children to receive education in a religious environment should not deprive them of their fair share of the public resources devoted to education."[16] In some places, home-schooled students are allowed to participate in band or sports opportunities offered in the public school. After all, there is an obvious problem with gathering people and resources for science labs, orchestras, tournaments, and computer technology when a school is limited to one or just a few families.[17]

Released time is another accommodation of the freedom of families to choose their children's education. Here the public school "releases" the child to go off-campus to a religious class during school hours. In some places, the student can even receive some types of credit for the time spent in the class, and the district can receive funding for the hours spent off campus.[18]

We will continue to see ever-changing ideas that allow public and private schools to work together to educate children and honor differing religious beliefs. These changes are all coming about because Americans are free to think creatively about schools. As one author said,

> Whether we like it or not, tax-funded education is losing its vitality. Its real enemy is not any particular pressure group or ideological faction. The public schools are being driven toward extinction by the flowering of democracy itself."[19]

Many people are interested in the idea of getting

financial aid to help make choices about their children's education. After all, some people ask, if President Clinton, Senator Edward Kennedy, and movie mogul Steven Spielberg can send their children to private schools, why should the less fortunate not have that opportunity as well?

There are some who disagree, however. They fear that with public money offered to set up private schools, unqualified amateurs will decide to attempt to educate children.[20] They also have concerns that tax funds will be "raided," leaving little for some less glamorous but still worthy programs. Schools, however, are funded by laws made by individual states. Most fund public schools by giving a school district a set amount, say, six thousand dollars per pupil enrolled. Thus, if a given school lost ten students to a private school, it would lose sixty thousand dollars. But these laws can be changed. If voters could agree not to fund by counting students, but per school, or on the basis of need or academic success, then public schools would not need to fear competition from private schools. The laws awarding funding can be more creative in the future.

There are new ideas emerging about financing public education. Many school districts are coming up with fresh ideas about forming partnerships with

The Capitol in Washington D.C., where the Congress meets to write bills, is shown here. The Constitution says, "Congress shall make no law respecting an establishment of religion, nor prohibiting the free exercise thereof."

corporate sponsors, soliciting private donations of money or services, offering effective fund-raising events, and selling bonds, which can bring in millions of dollars. Costs can be lowered, too. Allowing part-time faculty positions, as colleges do, or contracting out cafeteria services to the lowest private bidder, are two examples.[21]

More and more, the Establishment Clause issues that have divided and confused us in the school context are becoming more a matter of seeing schools as a forum for expression and a sharing of ideas, rather than seeing schools as a pipeline of state funds. If that forum is kept diverse, and fair, students can learn and arrive at truth for themselves. The Equal Access Act is a federal law. It says that if a public school allows any extra-curricular clubs, it must allow student-led religious clubs to operate on campus.[22] These clubs must be allowed access to the school bulletin board, public address system, and yearbook just like other clubs. In *Rosenberger* v. *University of Virginia*, a Christian student newspaper was held to have been a victim of "viewpoint discrimination" when school activity fees were parceled out to other groups but not that paper.[23]

With people on all sides of the issues in education, speaking up and handling problems in an honest and open-minded way, we will be able to live together peacefully and productively. We can close with the words of a high school student:

> Respect requires some knowledge about people's backgrounds. Singing Christmas carols as a kid in school did not make me Christian, but it taught me to appreciate beautiful music and someone else's holiday. It's not necessary or desirable for all ethnic groups in America to assimilate into one traditionless mass. Rather, we all need to learn about other cultures so that we can understand one another and not feel threatened by others.[24]

Questions for Discussion

Take these fact situations and consider how you would handle them. Then see the Comments section at the end.

1. Emily and Timothy Hsu, student founders of a Bible club at a public high school, sued the school district for failing to officially recognize their club as it did other clubs. The school had rejected the Bible club requirement that all club members and officers be "professed Christians." Officer positions were coordinator of activities, secretary, music coordinator, vice president, and president. The school had a policy of not allowing "discrimination" in school clubs.

   Would the school be "establishing religion" if it allowed this club to be exempt from the policy? Would it be violating the "Equal Access Act" if it denied recognition to the group? (The Equal Access Act guarantees that student-led religious clubs will be treated like all other clubs at public high schools that have other clubs.) Is the answer different for members than for officers? Would the answer be different if we were talking about a private school? How about a public elementary school?

2. University professor Dr. Dilip Chaudhuri taught at a university where prayers were once offered at university functions such as faculty meetings and graduation. In some situations, this practice was stopped and a moment of silence was substituted. At other times, a "generic, nonsectarian" prayer was offered. The professor sued, saying that the intent was still to continue prayer. Does it matter that it was a college-level student body? Does Dr. Chaudhuri have standing? (See page 34.)

3. The Salvation Army, an international Christian religious and charitable organization, terminated a woman from her job there, claiming a need to downsize. She went to the state for unemployment payments, but the Salvation Army said they were exempt from the laws governing payment of unemployment benefits. The *Lemon* test was applied. What do you think was the result? What other facts would you need to know to be sure?

4. A small public school in a rural area happens to be attended only by children from a religious sect. These people believe, among other things, that computers are objectionable and do not allow their children to use them. These children would otherwise be home-schooled, but the parents are willing to have a public-school teacher be bused to their area. Does this small school create an Establishment Clause problem? Can the district accommodate the parents' objections to computers?

Comments

1. *Hsu* v. *Roslyn Union Free School District,* No. 3, 85 F. 3d 839 (2d Cir. 1996) said that the president, vice president, and music coordinator of the club could be required to be Christians so that the type of speech the club wanted could be ensured. The other restrictions, however, were discriminatory. The school had to give unconditional recognition to the club once it dropped the restrictions. A private school does not have to comply with the Equal Access Act. Elementary schools are not named in the Equal Access Act.

2. Judges are less concerned about college students being made to think that the state is promoting religion or coercing them than about younger, more impressionable children. Dr. Chaudhuri definitely has standing if he has witnessed any of the offending events. He might have a tougher time if he had not.

3. *Rojas* v. *Fitch,* 127 F. 3d 184 (1st Cir. 1997) held that the law allowing religious groups out of the unemployment system was not "entirely motivated by a purpose to advance religion." Therefore, it did not cause an establishment of religion under *Lemon.* The court also said such exemptions serve a secular purpose: reducing the difficulty of administering the state's unemployment system (by leaving out many organizations). This last reason probably will not hold up outside the First Circuit.

4. A federal appeals court ruled in *Stark* v. *Independent School District* that under a classic *Lemon* analysis, the rural school could be funded. It was less expensive to bus

one teacher to the children than to bus nineteen children to the next-nearest school. The economic and educational motives of the district were suitable secular purposes. The allocation of aid to the students was based on neutral, secular criteria, and so did not advance religion. Further, the school was not any more entangled in religion than if the students attended a larger public school and wanted accommodation there for their beliefs.

Chapter Notes

Chapter 1. Close Questions

1. Author interview with Barbara Drew, April 11, 1997.

2. Author interview with Dan Woska, November 14, 1998.

3. *Zobrest* v. *Catalina Foothills School District,* 509 U.S. 1 (1993).

4. *Abington* v. *Schempp,* 374 U.S. 203, 230 (1963). Concurrence of Justice Brennan.

5. New Testament, Matthew 6:24, Matthew 22:21.

6. Author interview with Deal Hudson, February 5, 1997.

7. Author interview with Jane Waldorf, January 19, 1999.

8. *Tinker* v. *Des Moines,* 393 U.S. 503 (1969).

9. Harvey Fireside and Sarah Betsy Fuller, *Brown* v. *Board of Education: Equal Schooling for All* (Hillside, N.J.: Enslow Publishers, Inc., 1994), pp. 89–90.

10. Phillip J. Cooper, "Justice William O. Douglas: Conscience of the Court," in Charles M. Lamb and Stephen C. Halpern, *The Burger Court: Political and Judicial Profiles* (Urbana, Ill.: University of Illinois Press, 1991), p. 167.

11. Charles M. Lamb, "Chief Justice Warren E Burger: A Conservative Chief for Conservative Times," in Charles M. Lamb and Stephen C. Halpern, *The Burger Court: Political and Judicial Profiles* (Urbana, Ill.: University of Illinois Press, 1991), pp. 130, 132.

12. Kermit L. Hall, ed., *The Oxford Companion to the Supreme Court* (New York: Oxford University Press, 1992), p. 105.

Chapter 2. The Evolution of American Education

1. Lawrence Kotin and William Aikman, *Legal Foundations of Compulsory School Attendance* (Port Washington, N.Y.: Kennikat Press, 1980), p. 9; Martin Fritz, "Why Public Schools Cannot Be Reformed," *Crisis in Education*, February 1998, p. 46.

2. Kotin and Aikman, p. 17.

3. Ibid.

4. *The Code of 1650, Being a Compilation of the Earliest Laws and Orders of the General Court of Connecticut* (Hartford, Conn.: Silus Andrus, 1822), pp. 92–93.

5. Verna Hall and Rosalie Slater, *The Bible and the Constitution* (San Francisco: Foundation for American Christian Education, 1996), p. 28.

6. William H. McGuffey, *McGuffey's Eclectic Fourth Reader* (Cincinnati: Winthrop B. Smith & Co, 1853), p. 3, preface.

7. James Madison, "Letter to the Reverend Jaspar Adams" in Daniel L. Dreisbach, *Real Threat and Mere Shadow: Religious Liberty and the First Amendment* (Wheaton, Ill.: Crossway Books, 1987), p. 191.

8. James Madison, "Detached Memoranda," Elizabeth Fleet, ed., "Madison's Detached Memoranda," *The William and Mary Quarterly*, 534 (3rd Series, 1946).

9. "Regulations Adopted by the Board of Visitors of the University of Virginia, October 4, 1824," Saul K. Padover, ed., *The Complete Jefferson* (New York: Tudor Publishing Company, 1943), p. 1110.

10. Gerald Gutek, *Education in the United States* (Englewood Cliffs, N.J.: Prentice Hall, Inc., 1986), p. 30.

11. John W. Whitehead and Alexis Irene Crow, *Home Education: Rights and Reasons* (Wheaton: Ill.: Crossway Books, 1993), pp. 38–41.

12. Ibid., p. 43.

13. John D. Pulliam, *History of Education in America* (New York: Macmillan, 1991), p. 91.

14. Gutek, p. 118.

15. Whitehead and Crow, pp. 46–47, 54.

16. Stephen Bates, *Battleground: One Mother's Crusade, the Religious Right, and the Struggle for Control of Our Classrooms* (New York: Simon & Schuster, 1993), pp. 46–47.

17. Ibid., p. 43.

18. John Eidsmoe, *The Christian Legal Advisor* (Grand Rapids, Mich.: Baker Book House, 1984), p. 211.

19. Author interview with Rabbi Samuel Joseph, Professor of Jewish Education, Hebrew Union College, December 1, 1998.

20. Ibid.

21. *Zorach* v. *Clauson*, 343 U.S. 306 (1952).

22. Bates, pp. 46–47.

23. Ibid., p. 48.

24. *Engel* v. *Vitale*, 370 U.S. 421 (1962).

25. Bates, p. 47.

26. Ibid., p. 48.

27. Ibid., p. 49.

28. *Abington* v. *Schempp*, 374 U.S. 203 (1963).

29. West Virginia Board of *Education* v. *Barnette*, 319 U.S. 624 (1943); *Tinker* v. *Des Moines School District*, 393 U.S. 503 (1969); "Clinton: Prayer already OK in schools," Honolulu Star-Bulletin, July 12, 1995, p. 1A.

30. W. W. Sweet, *Religion in the Development of American Culture* (New York: Peter Smith, 1963), p. 50.

31. Thomas Barnes, *The Book of the General Lawes and Libertyes Concerning the Inhabitants of the Massachusetts* (San Marino, Calif.: The Huntington Library, 1975), p. A-2; Massachusetts School Law of 1642, *Records of the Governor and Company of Massachusetts Bay in New England* (June 14, 1642), pp. 6, 7.

32. *Maynard* v. *Hill*, 125 U.S 190, 206 (1888).

33. *Meyer* v. *Nebraska*, 262 U.S. 390, 403 (1923).

34. *Pierce* v. *Society of Sisters*, 268 U.S. 510, 534–5 (1925).

35. *Farrington* v. *Tokushige*, 273 U.S. 284 (1927).

36. *Griswold* v. *Connecticut*, 381 U.S. 479 (1965); *Roe* v. *Wade*, 410 US. 113 (1973)

Chapter 3. The Lawsuit Begins

1. *Lemon* v. *Kurtzman*, 403 U.S. 602 at 609–610 (1971).

2. Author interview with Henry W. Sawyer III, December 7, 1998.

3. *Lemon* v. *Kurtzman*, p. 603; William Bentley Ball, "Secularism: Tidal Wave of Repression," in Michael Cromartie, ed., *Caesar's Coin Revisited*, (Washington, D.C.: The Ethics and Public Policy Center and Eerdmans Publishing Co., 1996), p. 49; John Eidsmoe, *The Christian Legal Advisor* (Grand Rapids, Mich.: Baker Book House, 1984), p. 281.

4. Author interview with Henry W. Sawyer III, December 7, 1998.

5. *Lemon* v. *Kurtzman*, p. 608.

6. Author interview with Milton Stanzler, December 7, 1998.

7. Ibid.

8. Ibid.

9. Ibid.

10. Author interview with Henry W. Sawyer III, December 7, 1998.

11. Bernard Schwartz, *The Ascent of Pragmatism: The Burger Court in Action* (Reading, Mass.: Addison-Wesley Publishing Co., Inc., 1990), p. 191.

12. Ibid.

13. Ibid.

14. Ibid.

15. Ibid.

16. *Tilton* v. *Richardson*, 403 U.S. 672 (1971).

17. Schwartz, p. 193.

18. Ibid., pp. 193, 199.

19. Ibid., p. 193.

20. Ibid., p. 191.

21. Ibid., p. 192; Bob Woodward and Scott Armstrong, *The Brethren: Inside the Supreme Court* (New York: Simon & Schuster, 1979), pp. 44, 63.

22. Woodward and Armstrong, pp. 48–49, 53, 64.

Chapter 4. Justice Burger and His Court

1. Bob Woodward and Scott Armstrong, *The Brethren: Inside the Supreme Court* (New York: Simon & Schuster, 1979), p. 14.

2. Ibid.

3. Ibid.

4. Ibid., p. 17.

5. Ibid., p. 21.

6. Henry J. Abraham, *Justices and Presidents: A Political History of Appointments to the Supreme Court* (New York: Oxford University Press, 1985), p. 296.

7. Ibid., pp. 294–295; Charles M. Lamb and Stephen C. Halpern, eds., *The Burger Court: Political and Judicial Profiles* (Urbana: University of Illinois Press, 1991), pp. 11, 130.

8. Interview with Henry W. Sawyer, December 7, 1998; Yale Kamisar, "The Warren Court, The Burger Court, and Police Investigatory Practices" in Vincent Blasi, ed., *The Burger Court: The Counter-Revolution That Wasn't* (New Haven, Conn.: Yale University Press, 1983), p. 79.

9. Blasi, p. ix.

10. Ibid., p. xii.

11. Francis Graham Lee, *Neither Liberal Nor Conservative: The Burger Court on Civil Rights and Liberties* (Malabar, Fla.: Robert E. King Publishing Company, 1983), p. 67.

12. Blasi, p. xiii.

13. Ibid., pp. 5, 14, 33, 47, 49.

14. Kermit L. Hall, *The Oxford Companion to the Supreme Court* (New York: Oxford University Press, 1992), p. 104.

15. Ibid.

16. Woodward and Armstrong, pp. 29–31.

17. Abraham, p. 299.

18. Ibid., pp. 299–300.

19. Herman Schwartz, *The Burger Years, Rights and Wrongs in the Supreme Court 1969–1986* (New York: Viking Penguin Inc., 1987), pp. xii–xiii.

20. Ibid.

21. Woodward, pp. 54, 58–59.

22. Hall, p. 105.

23. Stephen L. Wasby, "Justice Harry A. Blackmun: Transformation from 'Minnesota Twin' to Independent Voice," in Lamb and Halpern, p. 70.

24. Woodward, p. 173.

25. Lamb and Halpern, p. 31.

26. Philip J. Cooper, "Justice William O. Douglas: Conscience of the Court," in Lamb and Halpern, p. 168.

27. Ibid.

28. Ibid.

29. Wallace Mendelson, "Justice John Marshall Harlan: Non sub Homine . . . .", in Lamb and Halpern, p. 194.

30. *Walz* v. *Tax Commission*, 397 U.S. 664 (1970).

31. Hunter R. Clark, *Justice Brennan: The Great Conciliator* (New York: Carol Publishing Group, 1995), p. 187.

32. Ibid.

33. Woodward and Armstrong, pp. 73–74, 137, 217, 222, 243.

34. Abraham, pp. 270–271, 277.

35. *Abington* v. *Schempp*, 374 U.S. 203, 312 (1963).

36. Tinsley E. Yarbrough, "Justice Potter Stewart: Decisional Patterns in Search of Doctrinal Moorings," in Lamb and Halpern, p. 376.

37. William J. Daniels, "Justice Thurgood Marshall: The Race for Equal Justice," in Lamb and Halpern, p. 213.

38. Ibid., p. 235.

39. Blasi, p. 247.

40. *Board of Education* v. *Allen*, 392 U.S. 236, 612 (1968).

41. *Everson* v. *Board of Education,* 330 U.S. 1, 15–16 (1947).

42. Howard Ball, "Justice Hugo L. Black: The Enduring Effort to Realize Law Over Judicial Discretion," in Lamb and Halpern, pp. 35, 36, 38.

Chapter 5. The Ruling

1. *Board of Education* v. *Allen,* 392 U.S. 326 (1968); Everson v. Board of Education, 330 U.S. 1 (1947).

2. *Walz* v. *New York Tax Commission,* 397 U.S. 664 (1970); Bernard Schwartz, The Ascent of Pragmatism: The Burger Court in Action (Reading, Mass.: Addison-Wesley Publishing Co., Inc., 1990), p. 75.

3. *Lemon* v. *Kurtzman,* 403 U.S. 602, 624 (1971).

4. Ibid., p. 617.

5. Ibid., p. 613.

6. Interview with Henry W. Sawyer III, December 7, 1998.

7. *Lemon* v. *Kurtzman,* p. 634.

8. Herman Schwartz, *The Burger Years, Rights and Wrongs in the Supreme Court 1969–1986* (New York: Viking Penguin Inc., 1987), p. 190.

9. Ibid., p. 120.

10. Ibid.

11. Charles M. Lamb and Stephen C. Halpern, eds., *The Burger Court: Political and Judicial Profiles* (Urbana: University of Illinois Press, 1991), p. 31; Henry J. Abraham, *Justices and Presidents,* 2nd ed. (New York: Oxford University Press, 1985), p. 265.

12. *Lemon* v. *Kurtzman,* p. 604.

13. Ibid.

14. Ibid., p. 612.

15. Ibid., p. 613.

16. Ibid.

17. Ibid., p. 614.

18. Ibid., pp. 616–617.

19. Ibid., p. 617.

20. Ibid., pp. 617, 619, 621.

21. Ibid., p. 622.

22. Ibid., p. 623.

23. Ibid., p. 625.

24. Ibid., p. 636, quoting L. Boettner, Roman Catholicism 375, 1962.

25. Ibid., p. 635.

26. Ibid., p. 643.

27. Ibid.

28. Ibid., p. 645.

29. Ibid.

30. Ibid., pp. 646–647.

31. Ibid., p. 663.

32. Ibid., p. 670.

33. Ibid., p. 671.

34. Ibid., p. 670.

35. Jacob Landynski, "Justice Lewis F. Powell, Jr.: Balance Wheel of the Court," in Lamb and Halpern, p. 277.

36. Sue Davis, "Justice William Rehnquist: Right Wing Ideologue or Majoritarian Democrat?" in Lamb and Halpern, pp. 315–316.

37. Kermit Hall, ed., *The Oxford Companion to the Supreme Court* (New York: Oxford University Press, 1992), p. 398.

38. Davis, p. 318.

39. *Lemon* v. *Kurtzman*, 93 S. Ct 1463, 1469 (1973).

40. Ibid., p. 1473.

41. Ibid., p. 1470.

Chapter 6. The Impact of the Case

1. Interview with Henry W. Sawyer III, December 7, 1998.

2. Wallace Mendelson, "Justice John Marshall Harlan: Non sub Homine . . . ", in Charles M. Lamb and Stephen C. Halpern, *The Burger Court: Political and Judicial Profiles* (Urbana, Ill.: University of Illinois Press, 1991), p. 196.

3. Lee Epstein et al., *The Supreme Court Compendium: Data, Decisions, and Developments* (Washington, D.C.: Congressional Quarterly, 1994), p. 604.

4. Ronald Kahn quoted in Kermit Hall, ed., *The Oxford Companion to the Supreme Court* (New York: Oxford University Press, 1992), p. 500.

5. Leonard Levy quoted in Hall, p. 500.

6. Kahn, p. 500.

7. Vincent Blasi, *The Burger Court: The Counter-Revolution That Wasn't* (New Haven, Conn.: Yale University Press, 1983), p. 214.

8. Ibid., p. 215.

9. Ibid., p. 216.

10. Herman Schwartz, *The Burger Years: Rights and Wrongs in the Supreme Court, 1969–1986* (New York: Viking Penguin Inc., 1987), p. 60.

11. *Lemon* v. *Kurtzman*, 403 U.S. 602, 612-613 (1971).

12. Schwartz, p. 61.

13. *Larkin* v. *Grendel's Den*, Inc. 459 U.S. 116 (1982).

14. Bernard Schwartz, *The Ascent of Pragmatism: The Burger Court in Action* (Reading, Mass.: Addison-Wesley Publishing Co., Inc., 1990), p. 200.

15. Ibid.

16. *Lynch* v. *Donnelly*, 465 U.S. 688 (1984).

17. *Marsh* v. *Chambers*, 463 U S.783 (1983).

18. Schwartz, p. 203.

19. Ibid.

20. *Marsh* v. *Chambers*, 465 U.S. 668, 711–712 (1983).

21. Bernard Schwartz, p. 204.

22. Ibid.

23. Ibid., pp. 75–77.

24. Ibid., p. 75.

25. Ibid., p. 76.

26. *Aguilar* v. *Felton*, 473 U.S. 385 (1985); *Zobrest* v. *Catalina Foothills School District*, 509 U.S. 1, 14, 18 (1993).

27. Aguilar, pp. 386–389, 391, 393.

28. *Agostini* v. *Felton*, 521 U.S. 203 (1997).

29. Tamara Henry, "Religious Guidance: Clinton Directive Tries to Clarify Activities Allowed," *USA Today*, August 22, 1995, p. 4D.

30. *Lee* v. *Weisman*, 505 U.S. 577 (1992).

31. *Jones* v. *Clear Creek Independent School District*, 977 F. 2d 963 (5th Cir. 1992), cert denied, 113 S. Ct. 2950 (1993); *Adler* v. *Duval City School Board*, 851 F. Supp. 446 (M.D. Fla. 1994); but see *ACLU* v. *Black Horse Pike Regional Board of Education*, 84 F. 3d 1471 (3d Cir. 1996).

32. *Lamb's Chapel* v. *Center Moriches Union Free School District*, 508 U.S. 304 (1993).

33. *Rosenberger* v. *Rector and Visitors of the University of Virginia*, 515 U.S. 819 (1995).

34. *Stone* v. *Graham*, 449 U.S. 39 (1980).

35. *Kolodziej* v. *Smith and Electro-Term*, Inc., U.S. Supreme Court Docket No. 97, 1998; *Frasee* v. *Illinois Department of Employment Security*, 489 U.S. 829 (1989).

36. *Witters* v. *Washington Department of Services for the Blind*, 474 U.S. 481 (1997).

37. *County of Allegheny* v. *ACLU*, 492 U. S. 573, 631 (1989); *Capitol Square Review* v. *Pinette*, 515 U.S. 753 (1995).

38. *Lee* v. *Weisman*, 505 U.S. 577 (1992).

39. *Church of Lukumi Babalu Aye, Inc.*, v. *City of Hialeah*, 508 U.S. 520, 1993.

40. *Marsh* v. *Chambers*, 463 U.S. 783 (1983).

41. *Lamb's Chapel* v. *Center Moriches*, Ibid.

42. *Church of Lukumi Babalu Aye* v. *City of Hialeah*, p. 520.

43. *Mueller* v. *Allen*, 463 U.S. 388 (1983)

44. *Lynch* v. *Donnelly*, 465 U.S. 668 (1984).

45. *Rosenberger* v. *Rector and Visitors of the University of Virginia*, ibid.

46. *Helms* v. *Picard*, 151 P. 3d 347, 362 (5th Cir. 1998), quoting *Agostini* v. *Felton* 117 S. Ct. 2016.

47. *Lamb's Chapel* v. *Center Moriches*, concurrence, pp. 1–3.

48. Ibid.

49. Ibid.

Chapter 7. Beyond *Lemon*

1. Dr. George Roche, *Imprimis*, October 1994, vol. 23, no. 10, p. 1.

2. Author Interview with Dennis Queen, July 10, 1997.

3. Robert L. Cord, *Separation of Church and State: Historical Fact and Current Fiction* (Grand Rapids, Mich.: Baker Book House, 1988), pp. 181–182.

4. Mindy Belz, "Finding Their Voice," *World*, October 3, 1998, p. 23; Nina Shea, *In the Lions' Den* (Nashville, Tenn.: Broadman & Holman Publishers, 1997), p. 25.

5. Robert L. Maginnis, "Voters Assess Drug Policy," *Washington Watch*, March 1998, p. 8.

6. ABC *World News Tonight*, "Education," January 9, 1997.

7. Claudio Sanchez, "All Things Considered," National Public Radio, January 19, 1999; "How a 900 Percent Increase in Youth Crime Was Reduced by 25 Percent" (Indianapolis, Ind.: *Newsletter of the Institute in Basic Life Principles*, March 1998), p. 3.

8. Joel Kilpatrick, "Jesus Movement," *Charisma*, November 1998, p. 124; John Leland, "Savior of the Streets," *Newsweek*, June 1, 1998, p. 20.

9. *Church on the Rock* v. *City of Albuquerque*, 84 F. 3d 1273 (10th Cir. 1997).

10. Maginnis, p. 8.

11. Thomas Toch and Warren Cohen, "Public Education: A Monopoly No Longer: A Chance to Choose the School You Want," *U.S. News and World Report*, November 23, 1998, p. 25.

12. *Committee for Public Education* v. *Nyquist*, 413 U. S. 756, 782–783, 1973.

13. "Outstanding High Schools," *U.S. News & World Report*, January 18, 1999, p. 75.

14. John W. Whitehead and Alexis Irene Crow, *Home Education: Rights and Reasons* (Wheaton, Ill.: Crossway Books, 1993), p. 381.

15. Barbara Kantrowitz and Pat Wingert, "Learning at Home: Does It Pass the Test?" *Newsweek*, October 5, 1998, p. 66.

16. Mark McConnell, "Unconstitutional Implications of the Establishment Clause," *San Diego Law Review 255*, p. 268.

17. Interview with attorney Dan Woska, December 9, 1998.

18. *Zorach* v. *Clauson*, 343 U.S. 306, 1952; *Lanner* v. *Wimmer*, 662 F. 2d 1349 (1981).

19. James L. Payne, "Education versus the American Way," *National Review*, September 25, 1995, p. 62.

20. Sanchez, p. 3.

21. "Outstanding High Schools," p. 67.

22. *Westside Community Schools* v. *Mergens*, 496 U.S. 226, 1990.

23. 115 Supreme Court Reporter 2510, 1995.

24. Chana Schoenberger, "Getting to Know About You and Me," in Charles Haynes and Oliver Thomas, eds., *The Freedom Forum First Amendment Center*, 1996, pp. 7–12.

Glossary

abridge—To limit.

agnostic—A person who neither denies nor believes in the existence of God.

atheism—The belief that there is no God. For purposes of free speech and protection of freedom of conscience under the Constitution, this belief qualifies as a religion.

bench—Judges or justices (as opposed to the bar, which refers to attorneys); the judiciary.

concurrence—A written opinion by a Justice who agrees with the majority but wants to add additional or different reasoning.

dissent—A written opinion disagreeing with the majority.

injunction—Order by a court, usually to stop an activity.

litigation—The process of trying a lawsuit.

parochial—Religious in nature. Literally "from a parish."

precedent—Previous case law.

sectarian—Religious. Sometimes refers to religious sects or subgroups.

secular—Nonreligious.

Further Reading

Books

Cord, Robert L. *Separation of Church and State: Historical Fact and Current Fiction*. Grand Rapids, Mich.: Baker Book House, 1998.

Farish, Leah. *The First Amendment: Freedom of Speech, Religion, and the Press*. Springfield, N.J.: Enslow Publishers, Inc., 1998.

Hammond, Phillip E. *With Liberty For All: Freedom of Religion in the United States*. Louisville, KY.: Westminster John Knox Press, 1998.

Haynes, Charles C., and Oliver Thomas, eds. *Finding Common Ground: A First Amendment Guide to Religion and Public Education*. Nashville: The Freedom Forum First Amendment Center, 1994.

Hirst, Mike. *Freedom of Belief*. New York: Franklin Watts, Inc., 1997.

Jasper, Margaret C. *Religion and the Law*. Dobbs Ferry, N.Y.: Oceana Publications, Inc., 1998.

Lamb, Charles M. and Stephen C. Halpern. *The Burger Court: Political and Judicial Profiles*. Urbana, Il.: University of Illinois Press, 1991.

Internet Addresses

American Civil Liberties Union
<http://www.ACLU.org>
FreedomForum.org: First Amendment
<http://www.freedomforum.org/first>
The Oyez Project–Northwestern University
<http://oyez.nwu.edu/cases/cases.cgi>
Legal Information Institute–Cornell Law School
<http://www.law.cornell.edu>
The Rutherford Institute: Civil Liberties and Human Rights
<http://www.rutherford.org>

Index

MISSING OR
DAMAGED BAR[C]ODE
$5.00 FINE

DATE DUE
